The Psychology of Consciousness and Illusion: Reset Your Mind and Heart

Edited by
Georgia Estelle Gilbert
and
Ayon Leopold Valentine Skyers

Reset Your Mind and Heart

Psychology/Social Studies

Copyright

ISBN: 979-8-218-59006-2 (Paperback)

1st edition, January 2025

Published in the United States by Asarian and Astian

PART ONE

We are living in a World and Country and Culture that value stories. My story and your story deserve to be heard!

Dedication

This book is dedicated to those who have a reset heart and mind, to judge the truth and falsehood in an open market. Just so you know and pass on this knowledge to others. Don't be a coward because we all seek the free flow of knowledge.

Acknowledgements

It's your dignity, honor and rights, and my dignity, honor and rights to acknowledge some of the most wonderful and great inspirational Neter and Netert who promoted, supported and engaged in me. Who truly wants to see the Greatness of me and in me. And want to see this book published, to reset the mind and heart of all of us back to true consciousness.

And such acknowledgments go out to my beloved beautiful and loving father Herman Skyers (deceased) and mother Oddelee Skyers (deceased). And my best friends and loved ones such as: Vermalee Skyers, Elliston Skyers, Isaiah Gilbert, Diana Skyers, Thalia Campbell, Byron Hannah, and Jade-Ann Scott. My acknowledgements go out to all Alkebulan Neter and Netert throughout this cosmos, and to my publisher. Last but not least, to this acknowledgement is Patricia Ferguson.

Thank you all!

Table of Contents

Conclusion

Introduction

This book is about consciousness and illusion and how to reset your mind and heart. It embarks you down the road of the psychology of consciousness and illusion, the means by how and why you should not be deprived of how importantly it is to reset your mind and heart.

Our own Alkebulan knowledge teaches us that we cannot educate our mind and not educate our heart along with it. Thus, we got lost and carried away in these schools, colleges, universities, temples, synagogues, mosques, and churches that are owned and run by Nordic devils by not educating both our mind and heart.

And so, this wicked programming becomes a cycle, generation after generation of mindless and heartless wicked ones. We allow those who are heartless to play the role of a teacher, professor or scientist or even artist, to so-called educate us and our loved ones.

Learned behavior!

That's where we go in the incorrect way. Hence, it is at this junction, this book fills the vacuum to set things in line and order, for all.

My initial intent is to wake Alkebulan Neter and Netert up to the true knowledge of consciousness and illusion, and on how to reset your mind and heart, from which Nordic devil people indoctrinate, brainwash, and miseducate you all. Writing books like this one does not need your so-called slave masters and slave mistresses- Nordic devil people, certificates, degrees, titles, badges, and approvals. Our right of liberty guarantees the right to engage in any of the common occupations of life.

Hence, I have researched, and I did not see many books addressing the special needs to reset your mind and heart, not even to consciousness. After I have ascertained an iron cause to why this was so, I decided to offer my knowledge to fulfill this vacuum. It is we as the mature ones who must read this book and recommend it to our younger generation. Wake them up with it, to let them know and comprehend that we are the Neter and Netert and Artists and Scientists of this Cosmos.

We must not continue to act like animals and devils as how Nordic devil people program us to be like them. We are gifted as Neter and Netert, with a Divine Purpose to cleanse the Cosmos of the evil ones and wicked ones. Nordic devil people program us to the opposite.

Hence, we must teach the younger generation that the evil ones, and the wicked ones cannot be awakened nor enlightened, as this book will teach you. This is why it is good to know what consciousness means, to us. And that we can be awaken to consciousness, after we have been brainwashed, indoctrinated, miseducated, and programmed by Nordic devil people schools, colleges, universities, religions and social media. These mislead us from not knowing who and what we truly are.

They have not taught us that there are no limits to our ability and knowledge. We have not been taught that there are no limit to age. Aging is an illusion. However, all these schools, colleges, universities, temples, synagogues, mosques, churches, and social media have put limits on our knowledge, and on who and what we are, with their certificates, degrees, titles, and names. We were gifted with Divine Purpose. So, we do not need those stumbling blocks in our way to stop us from performing our Divine Purpose as Neter and Netert, and to stop us from eat and build.

We are gifted and we must utilize that gift by all means necessary. Neter and Netert do not need titles, degrees, and certificates to live and eat and build. Are we abandoning our Divine Gift as Neter and Netert and Artists and Scientists, to play stupid and ignorant for certificates, degrees, and titles? This ignorant and foolish idea of straying away from who and what we are, destroying and haunting our young loved ones, from generation to generation. All of this have them acting like animals and demons, cosmos wide.

Hence, I will try to use this book to reach out to you all to wake you all up to who and what you are, and who the devil truly is. Thus, let no one limit your ability. Therefore, I know that neither me, nor this book, nor no one else cannot change the psychology of none of you or educate you overnight. It did not take the devil and his trained disciples, long enough to use his schools, colleges, universities, Judaism, or Hebrewism, Christianity, and Islam to indoctrinate, brainwash, miseducate, program, and rob you of your true identity of who and what you are, and your Divine purpose.

So now why can't it take you all in the twinkling of an eye to wake you all up to who and what you are? Majority of the Earth population have been tricked to who and what they truly are. Have you not learnt yet that majority rule is an illusion? If majority rules, why then it's the least amount of Earth population control and have authority over the greater amount of the Earth's population? That's just one good example. Live in this cosmos with your eyes and ears open. Now, let's read, study, like, and share the truth of this book, to bring back the majority rule concept to true reality. Delve on into this book!

Chapter 1: Awakening to Who You Truly Are

Hello, and welcome!

I am excited for you to rediscover this amazing realization of who you truly are today. So please get comfortable and close your eyes for a moment of Transcendental Meditation, with some steel pan music, or jazz music, or whatever smooth Transcendental Meditation music of your own choice.

…. Cool, meditation music playing…

Ah, we are back!

Now with the power of your awareness become aware of the music in the background. No need to think about it. No need to judge it.

Just experience what it's like to be to just simple listen.

Okay, go ahead and listen to your music and meditate again.

Okay now if thoughts arrive pay them no mind. Your main focus is on listening, so play your music again.

Okay, now you can comprehend that you have a sense of being aware, right? You know what it feels like to be aware. But who is the one that is aware? It's not your male or female form, because you are aware of that also.

So, become aware and then become of your sense of awareness. Focus on the one who is aware. Notice that you are not your thoughts or feelings. Because you are aware of them.

1

Who you are cannot be answered mentally. Just experience being aware of your awareness.

Ah, meditate and listen to your music again.

Okay, now, if you are doing this correctly, thoughts will go away. But even if they are here, notice how they are at you.

Because you are that awareness. Behind every thought, behind every emotion, behind every single experience, you have been there this whole time. Behind your anxiety, and depression, and behind your fear, you have been there this whole entire time.

Isn't that so nice to hear?

You have never been alone.

This awareness that you are is always there and never left. When you start to suffer from anything, return back to becoming of your awareness, and notice that you are not the suffering. You are the one aware of it, and who you are have nothing to do with it, the one aware cannot be the one suffering. Because it is the one aware of the suffering.

You are not your body or mind, you are the awareness of the body and mind. The body and mind would not exist without you. Nothing exists without you. No matter what, challenge yourself to be more interesting in the one aware, instead of what you are aware of.

This age-old practice is by far the most important Divine practice. This is the key to real freedom! Now I will let you sink deep into this knowing along that I will revert with some more great knowledge after you meditate some more, with your music of choice. Knowing that Transcendental Meditation is the most important Divine practice.

Oh yes, now you're back from your meditation!

To give you my final thoughts on awakening to who you truly are.

So how was your experience?

I want you to realize that you are everything, nothing can exist without you. You were here before you were born, and you will be here after this male or female body is gone!

You are Light!

You are a Neter!

You are a Netert!

Neter is within you!

Netert is within you!

My Being is your Being.

We all share the same awareness. My awareness is not different from yours. Everything is connected. Don't search for happiness because you are happiness. Your peace loves confidence, it's your natural state of Being.

This knowledge will grow deeper and deeper the more you return back to this essence of you.

You are spaciousness. You are this open space of consciousness, where everything can come and go as you allow them to be. You are a Powerful Being, a Powerful Creator.

You are the Creator.

Thank you so much for reading this!

Just because your eyes are now open doesn't mean that you are to stop meditating.

You are Meditation.

And that's transcendental meditation equal Pure Consciousness.

On the word: Neter, they taught in their schools, colleges, universities and academic of theology that you must not translate names, but yet they translate the name Neter to be God. Moses must remain Moses. Mount Sinai must remain Mount Sinai. Neter must remain Neter.

We do not like the word 'God' because it is the Germanic/Dutch, and why use Germanic/Dutch when we have the ancient Alkebulan word Neter, which to our ears is quite as euphonious, if not more so.

Consciousness is Neter and Netert!

Awareness is Neter and Netert!

And you are Neter and Netert!

The word God or Gods is an illusion.

Chapter 2: The Self Cannot Awaken, Self is an Illusion

I believe this chapter will benefit a lot of you, if you can realize what I am about to write and talk about. Because I believe it's where a lot of us hit a cast concrete wall during this journey to awakening.

Most of you reading this chapter and sharing this knowledge, actually have a lot of knowledge. You can probably teach these teachings. You have this mental comprehending of things. But because you aren't experiencing what you know, you're stuck in the seeking loop. You figure out something and then you feel like that's not enough, so you seek for more and more and more. And this can go on for trillions of days and days and days.

Some people have dedicated half of their lives seeking for that one piece of information that they believe will be the final thing they need to know to realize their true nature. And the funny thing is usually when they find a new piece of information it's something they have already know. It's just word it different or there is still this belief that it's not true, but they want it to be so bad.

If this is you right now, it's okay! Because today is the end of all of that madness now. But let me explain why this confusion and seeking energy stays around. To sum it all up, it's only because you believe that the false self can awaken.

You truly believe that a man and woman can awaken. You honestly believe that this mind and body will awaken. You believe that the character you believe yourself to be will finally understand something and awaken. But that's just another sneaky trick of the false self of the unconscious mind.

Because it's the false self that wants things. But it doesn't even exist. Isn't that funny? Who you believe yourself to be is just another thought. If you are hearing this for the first time, you probably think I'm crazy. But hey, news flash, you don't exist. I know that triggered some of those false selves.

Can't wait to see you making some irrational comments on social media about this book. But seriously you don't exist. There is just a belief that believes you are a male body or female body and the mind and it's not your fault for believing that. You have been told your whole life. You were conditioned into creating this mental character. If I ask you, who are you? You realize you have to pause and think about it. It's not real. It's all a mental creation.

Who you are can change. Because it's not and has never been real in the first place. But what you truly are cannot change or come and go. It's always here. Now why is this important to realize? Because how could the false self-awaken if it's not actually real?

So many of us are trying to awaken these mental created characters. When what you are is above all of it. It's not the false self that will awaken. It will be consciousness realizing that it's consciousness.

Consciousness will awaken to itself, consciousness.

You have taken form of billions of different body minds and have been playing a character who does not realize that its consciousness stuck in the mind illusions and false identifications.

So how do we realize this?

Well, whenever that seeking energy arises and there is an impulse to want something or to want to watch one hundred animated videos, realize the one who want, who, is it that wants something.

It can't be what I truly am, because I'm already everything. So that means it must be the false self that actually doesn't exist, who feels like it's not complete.

Now I'm not saying seeking energy is incorrect. Honestly seeking will stop when it's realized that no matter what concept or video or speech you attain, it will never get you closer to what is. So, if you continue seeking after this book it is okay. That's just what's happening. But if this book is for you, then take this to be an aligned message.

There is no such thing as a coincidence. Because you are everyone and everything. Here is a wow moment, listen to this.

You LED yourself to experience this very moment. Everything in life has LED you to this book.

You as in consciousness as trying to get itself to realize itself. Isn't that beautiful? This whole journey has been LED by you, but the false self is in the way of you realizing that.

Now this is also very important. Someone asked me: "Well how do I become consciousness, no matter how hard I try I just can't seem to experience those glimpses people talk about?" And I said trying is the reason why you haven't realized it. We are so used to trying things and working hard for things to get something. That's what society condition and program and pushes us to do and believe, right? To work hard to achieve your goals and dreams. Chase your goals and dreams?

Chasing implies that something is running away from you, and you have to force yourself to catch it. How about attract your goals and dreams. And it's funny because the moment you give up trying to be consciousness, that's the very moment it will begin to shine through all the conditioning and through the false self. Consciousness is what you already are, you don't have to try to be it or try to see it. If this is our natural state, why is it that we believe we have to try to be natural. If you try to be natural that's pretty unnatural.

There is nothing you have to do sometime today, just sit and do nothing. Release all effort and just be! Don't identify with anything that arises. If you can do that, nothing will be able to distract you. You are not the mind, so let thoughts be. Don't follow them. You are not the body. So, allow whatever sensations to rise and go away. You don't need to imagine anything. Let that go also and you don't have to try to be the observer. You are always aware. If you weren't, the things that are rising wouldn't exist.

Do you see how you don't have to try to be what you already are? It's the only thing that's actually here. Everything else is a creation of the mind. The character you believe yourself to be is a creation of the mind. The past and the future are imaginary. They only exist in the mind. Because all we ever truly have is now!

Things you believe to be an issue only are perceived that way through the mind. This whole reality is literally a creation and illusion of the mind. Even what we call reality isn't what's actually happening. We cannot see what's actually happening. The mind is just so intelligent and magical that it's able to take in light and create what we perceive. The Universe is made up of ninety-nine percent empty space. We're just energy dancing around and things are just happening. There's nothing happening to nobody though. Things are just happening! That's the best way to explain it to you.

Now I regard this book to be written and read from what you truly are.

I don't care if the false self-comprehended this. It won't do anything for it but keep repeating knowledge to you. Thank you for happening.

However, the false self cannot comprehend because self is an illusion. We have no idea if this is real or not. We also have no idea if we actually exist or if this is all just some lucid dream. The only thing we know for certain is that we are aware. If I were to tell you that you don't exist, how would you respond to that? You would probably laugh at me and say well clearly, I do exist because I'm here, reading your writing telling me that I don't exist.

But you have no actual proof. The only thing you can say is that you are aware of this experience. This is the only thing that is one hundred percent true. Wouldn't it actually be pretty liberating to know that this is just a dream? That means we wouldn't have to take it so seriously.

Let's look at dreams for a moment. Because I really want you to comprehend that you don't really exist. I know it sounds a bit crazy. So when we are dreaming most of the scene, we cannot actually tell that we are dreaming. No matter what may be going on in the dream. For some reason we just accept it to be real during that experience. We can be dreaming about flying around like lizards that spit fire like a fake dragon.

And we don't question or realize that we are dreaming. We are so caught up in the experience that we don't even realize that we are dreaming. We can feel, taste, and hear. We have all of our five senses, dreaming the same exact way we do when we are so-called aware.

But just because we can sense those things doesn't mean it's real. Because obviously our bodies are just lying in bed and the dream is all happening in our head? So those senses can't really confirm consciousness. But the one thing we can confirm is that we are aware. We all always aware during our dream experience. If we weren't we would never know what dreaming is.

In fact, we can never not be aware. We may forget that we are aware. But we are always aware.

Now listen to this. We have bodies in those dreams, correct?

Hands, feet, and hear a voice.

The same exact way we have bodies while we are awake. But it's clear to you that the body you are using, and that dream wasn't real. The characters you are using in your dreams aren't real. And this also applies to the body you are of, while you are

10

awake. You are not your body. Look at your hands, that is not you.

You are not a human having a human body experience. You are consciousness, awareness experiencing this life experience as a Male and Female Being. It doesn't matter if this experience is real or not. You are still having an experience you are aware of we are consciousness.

Consciousness was here before you ever came out of your mother's womb to this planet called Earth and it will be here after. Male and Female Being do not create consciousness. Consciousness creates Male and Female Being. These characters that we have created is just consciousness expressing its Oneness. Consciousness is expressing everything and everyone. Because everything and everyone is created within this one consciousness. Do you see and comprehend what I am saying clearly?

Why when someone who is divinely enlightened, they say you are awake, you woke up. What are they awake from? What do you mean you woke up? Woke up from what? Well, what happens when we wake up from a crazy dream? We say oh wow, it was just a dream. And then we believe that we are awake. But we're not, because this is also a dream that we can wake up from. Are you following, right on? Hey, you are dreaming right now. I'm dreaming, you are dreaming, he's dreaming, she's dreaming. We are all having our own dreams inside of one big collective dream.

I mean really think about it. The law of Attraction and Manifestation is amazing. We can astro project. We create our own reality. Do you not see how truly powerful and amazing

11

we are. When you become aware that you are dreaming you can take a hold of your consciousness and do whatever you want in your dreams. It's called lucid dreaming. Where you can do the same exact thing in this so-called awakened state.

It's not called a Divine awakening for no reason. When you wake up you realize that this is not what it seems. And that this is basically just a dream. You realize that you are not this character and body. You are not your thoughts. You begin to realize that you are not a human experiencing the Universe. But instead, you are the Universe having a male and female experience. This is a very amazing realization.

It has completely changed my life and so many others. And the only reason why it may be so hard to see this to be true is because a human cannot awaken. Enlightenment cannot be achieved on a mental level, because a human cannot be awakened. You will be chasing this awakening for your whole life if you don't comprehend that awakening happens when you become aware of what you truly are. It's when consciousness becomes aware of its own awareness.

A human or monster or barbarian or person or devil are one and the same thing and cannot be aware of itself. Only awareness can be aware of itself. Try it for yourself. Try to make your body become aware of itself. It's not possible. The only thing that will happen will be you directing your awareness onto a sensation of the body. It's the awareness that is aware. It's not the human or the mind.

So, if you are on this journey of awakening, remember that your thoughts do not know who you are. And your body does not know who you are. Only you can know who you are. And this is why you can have all the knowledge in the world and still continue to suffer. Because thoughts cannot be you. To truly know who you are you must experience your Consciousness. You must become aware of your awareness.

Now, I'm not trying to make any of you dissociate and drive your consciousness crazy. I just want you all to enjoy this rediscover experience. With this knowledge you will be able to create the experience you wish to have. You can have anything you want. This is your dream and true Nature Way. This is your experience to play around with. If you would like more knowledge on this subject, research, non-duality and self-inquiry.

These two areas of study alone will lead you into the experience of knowing instead of this just being a belief and opinion. Also, if you have any issues or questions regarding your crutched life experience, please feel free to leave a comment on my community.

Email: ahaasar666@gmail.com.

You never know, I may choose you and create a full book surrounding your issue. Thank you for studying this to know that self is an illusion. Yet, here are some more food for thoughts. Santa Claus is an illusion, it's not real. Easter bunny is an illusion, it's not real. Mickey Mouse is an illusion, it's not real.

Yet look at the vast quantities of labor and day wage slavery put into them. Actors, roles, costumes, characters, and the many visits to some of them calling it fun and vacation.

Chapter 3: Detox Your Mind, the Mind Doesn't Know You

Grand rising my beloved. And hello, to you all.

I want to say to you all that what we called life is not what it is. But life is what we make out of it. And the one thing which either will make our life or break our life is our heart and mind!

Both go together. Now a days our hearts and minds are filled with stress, anxiety, worry and a general feeling of negativity. However, when we fill our heart and minds with such ideas and thoughts, we constantly add load, and load and load of extra pressure on our hearts and minds.

Think about it. It's like a balloon being stretched, and stretched, and stretched.

One day it is going to burst! But before that happens let's take a mental detox.

The first and foremost thing for our mental detox is having a peaceful and calm mind and heart. Hey, what better way to help you to achieve that than the Asarian and Astian principle of Transcendental Meditation. Transcendental Meditation is a simple way of life, but like most simple things, it is a powerful one. Transcendental Meditation means relaxation and recreation. Thus, the peaceful idea of Transcendental Meditation is deep rest, relaxation and reset for the heart and mind. This can be achieve through conscious efforts in activities that not only soothes, but also help the mind and heart to develop and regenerate its neutral networks.

So please try to develop hobbies and activities that challenge your mind and heart. Like, good diet, less crushing toiling, little exercise in the country area, Transcendental Meditation, dining, singing and gardening.

This will help you to get out of your mental loop of thoughts and make you conscious and centered and calm. More so, over time you may be even excited to do the things, inviting more joy and wholeness to your life. So stop delay. When there is so much more fun in getting your heart and mind detox. One thing for sure is that you cannot educate your mind and don't educate your heart too.

Up next, is to try and find out more than ten positive points before you sleep at night. Look, when you sleep you are slowing down the entire momentum of the day in your heart and mind.

You really have a chance to rewrite what your heart and mind focuses upon. So, when you go to sleep focusing on the positive things that happened to you during the day, automatically you train your heart and mind to look for positive things in your life. With such a conditioning you will slowly see changes. You will slowly see the entire outlook of your life changing.

Up next, two magic words, which most of the Neter and Netert don't Know is: Transcendental Meditation. It is most ignored by many of us. Oh yes, Transcendental Meditation will do wonders for you. Yet still we make a blunder of not having it in our regular daily routine. When you transcendentally meditate, you regenerate your heart and mind and recharge your body at the cellular level. Now, if you find it too difficult to transcendental meditate or you think that you don't have the time and energy, hear me out and put all of that filthy negative attitude aside and try Transcendental Meditation for once in your life.

Remember, that there is a first time for everything in every one of us life.

Thus, because what Transcendental Meditation can do for you in a minute, prayer and pharmaceutical medicine won't do it for you in your whole life span. And finally do not believe in any power that you were brainwashed to believe to be higher than you. You are the Neter and Netert the strongest, and greatest, and the most powerful power there is. Remember that your own power will never hurt you or harm you or do something that is bad for you. If you are going through something difficult always take it as a gift in disguise. And if you have lost something always know that you are being protected from what was never meant for you or would have harmed you. Look at it from any point of view you want to, a lot of our worries come from the belief that we live in an uncaring cold World. But remember that is not true. That is just our fear and anxious heart and mind talking. Remember that you are a Neter and Netert, and your consciousness is always there guarding your heart and mind to look out for you always.

Once you find the zeal and audacity to have this kind of consciousness and awareness you will not even need a Mental Detox. Because your heart and mind will always have peace and joy and happiness. Now remember to take care of your heart and mind, care for them well. Because how you care for your heart and mind will determine how well you lived your life. So why suffer, when you can thrive! That comes to the answer on how one detox their heart and mind.

The opening theme is that the mind doesn't know you and we will fathom down into this segment like this. When it comes to the realization of what we truly are, a lot of us have been directing our attention to the mind for answers. Yes, we go to the mind to find corroboration. But that's just another trick of the self-pride. Because the mind doesn't know you.

During your journey I am quite sure you have come across teachers or even in this work where I say you are consciousness, or you are Neter and Netert. Which is honestly true. But remember those are just titles and telling you that isn't meant for the mind to accept it and add it to its belief system. This is a no brainer. None of this knowledge is truly for the mind to ruminate over because it can't truly comprehend it anyway. This is why seeking for some can last for years simply because they believe the mind will awaken.

The mind believes that the mind needs more information to come to self-realization. And once again that is just another trick of the self-pride. It will put you in an endless loop that can last for many, many centuries. Self-realization happens when consciousness realizes itself as consciousness. It's not the false character that the mind has created you to believe to be that will awaken.

Thus, in other words it's not Diop that will awaken. Because Diop doesn't actually exist. It will be consciousness realizing its consciousness. I know for me at one point I had an image of what I thought I was. I had this image of consciousness, and I think a lot of us do this too. Whenever we

17

try to align with our true consciousness we tend to create this third Consciousness Being Vision. Where we vide our bodies from third Consciousness Being.

But that's not necessary. It's not necessary to have any kind of image of what you think you are.

Because that's just another creation of the mind.

We cannot create, we cannot imagine, we cannot vide or feel what we truly are. But the mind believes that we can. We have to realize seeking as another form of suffering at one point.

We have to realize that the mind will continue having you search for something that's already here. It's like someone has a sun cap on and their mind is saying we need to keep looking for the sun cap.

It's just that we don't believe that we are already what we seek. Maybe it's because we have a belief of how we think it should feel or how we think it should look. Realize that's also just the mind.

Thus, the mind has no clue it cannot be you. It wants to be you, but it can't.

The devil wants to be Neter and Netert. So it creates illusions to appear real. The self-pride wants to be consciousness So, it too, creates illusions to appear real.

Another thing that happened to me on this journey, was that I always tried to corroborate what I was, by repeating that I am consciousness, or I am not my thoughts, and I am not my body. But all that does is add something else to my belief

18

system. So you will once again run to the mind for corroboration. Don't add these to your belief system. You have to see this without the mind. If I say you aren't the body, see it, realize it, accept it without the mind. If I say you are not your thoughts, realize that you are that which is aware of thoughts arising.

You have to realize that you can't find what you are looking for, because you are already and have always been looking from it.

Running to the mind and depending on your knowledge for awakening can be a hard cycle to break. But the more you catch the mind seeking, the quicker this awakening will happen. You constantly ask yourself, when the mind starts to run to something, why isn't this moment enough. Knowing that this moment is literally everything.

How isn't it enough? And the mind may only have answered that question for you. But whatever it says is a lie. Hence, you don't need to feel happy to be what you are. Because what you truly are is behind feelings. How you feel doesn't matter. You don't need to feel like you are everything and everyone because you can never not be everything and everyone.

Regardless of how many stories the mind can create, separation doesn't exist. It's either it exists, or it doesn't. You can't go back and forth. That's what this all comes down to. It's either real or not real. Whatever the mind is saying isn't real, regardless of how real it feels. Fear isn't real, danger is. Separation isn't real, Oneness is.

However, the self-pride ultimately isn't real, but you are. You are the thing that's truly here. Everything is you, and you are Everything. I have heard and seeing a lot of you saying you want to comprehend this knowledge that I am teaching so bad or I'm so close to getting this knowledge. That's also just the mind and the reason a lot of this knowledge can get so confusing is because the mind tries to make sense out of something it can't. You will forever have that feeling of I am so close. But that's just another belief. Because you're already here.

And don't look for collaboration from the mind just realize it experience here. Whatever is present for you that is it.

Thus, I also was asked questions like how do I realize something without the mind or how do I experience without the mind.

However so, if you are someone who struggles with this I'd really recommend feeling into the body. For example, if I say experience the sensation we call the hand, you don't go thinking about the hand, you just feel it. You don't need to imagine it or create it. It's already here, all you have to do is experience it. The mind cannot feel. The mind cannot be. Thus, there may be thoughts about the feeling or the experience but simply remain focused on the experience. Once you get used to experiencing the body with the mind's distractions, you'll have a sense of how to simply be or how to experience what is. And the same applies to having realizations. Every realization you will have, comes from a direct experience. It doesn't come from an comprehending from the mind.

However, for example, if I say realize that you are not your thoughts, you can't use thoughts to realize that you can't say in your head, I am not my thoughts. That's just another thought. What was aware of that thought the same way you can listen to others speak, you can do the same when thoughts are rising. Just stop identifying with the voice that's rising in the mind of even externally. Because you're also not the voice. Letting go of the mind doesn't happen overnight. But it can have no expectations. It just takes constant inquire and awareness to see what's actually waiting to happen.

However, you'll begin to laugh at the mind when it tries to seek or figure out what you are. You'll see the stories and the BS it tries to create. And eventually you will transcend it. You'll begin to see that what's real exists outside of the mind, and outside of beliefs, outside of all concepts, and it's always been here. You have always been here everyone. You are the key. And that's the bottom line to the mind doesn't know you.

Cheer up!

Chapter 4: You're Not a Person

It's my duty to open your eyes and to enlighten you all to know that you're not a person. For many, many years so many of us try so hard to hold up this image. You have this image in your head of who you should be and you suffer from it. Because you're currently not this person. It's like you refuse to accept where and who you are in this moment, that you have plans for yourself. You have a future that you dream of constantly.

And for you to achieve those dreams you have to be the person that can make these dreams a reality. You can't have anxiety in the future. You can't be depressed while chasing your dreams. Yes, right now this is your current experience. You're stressing yourself out and causing unnecessary suffering. Don't fall victim to the illusion of the future. The future only exists within the mind. Not once in your experience have you ever experienced the future.

Thus, you have always been here, and if you can't accept this moment you will forever procrastinate. You will forever believe that you have time, and you will continue chasing this personality and vision of who you want to be. And do you know what's funny is, everyone is just looking for an escape from themselves.

Everyone is tired of holding up being these characters. And the best thing about this is when you come to self-realization, you will realize that you were never this person to begin with. You have to stop trying to be someone. It's why you're overthinking everything and every conversation.

It's why you believe you need things from this external world to truly be Free. You must stop trying to be a person.

Hence, what does that really mean though?

How could you stop trying to be a person, how would you function in society and how could you take care of your responsibilities and relationships, how do you chase your dreams? Well, Well, Well, you have to first comprehend that the person you want to be or the person you believe yourself to be today is simply an illusion. It's a creation of the mind. Even though it feels real and appears real, it's honestly just a filter over reality.

You are pretending to be a person. But you have been pretending for so long that you grew an attachment to this idea, and also began identifying with it. You are Neter and Netert. But you just forgot. The person doesn't actually exist. What is your person's name? Say your name is Jennifer. Okay, so just realize what I am about to say Jennifer, that is the title or name, or label given to the vessel that Neter is experiencing. Jennifer has a life story, correct? Jennifer has these wants and needs, these desires, Jennifer has belief.

Jennifer claims to be the thinker of thoughts and the feeler of emotions. However, Jennifer also claims to have a body or Jennifer claims to be the body.

But where does this idea of Jennifer exist?

Where is Jennifer?

Well Jennifer would say I'm right here. Jennifer would say here I am in the flesh that's very clear to realize. Yes, I am Jennifer. You cannot find Jennifer anywhere. You are not the body. You have to realize this, that the body is something within you. You are not within the body. The body is within awareness. Can you realize this right now? It's an object that you as Neter, as awareness is aware of. Therefore it cannot be you. You are the subject. You could play a game with yourself.

Everything you are aware of, label it, and object and affirm that it cannot be you.

Knowing that Jennifer doesn't exist and has never existed, will set you Free. You said, how would that set you Free? You don't get it. Well Jennifer is the one who has anxiety, right? Jennifer is the one who is depressed, right? Jennifer is the one who allows the illusion of the past to define what you are, right? Yes! Wow you're starting to comprehend. Jennifer is the One who claims these things. The one who appears to hold on to things. Even the one who appears to be the thinker of thoughts?

But isn't Jennifer just another thought, just another idea? Holy shit! Okay, but how do you disconnect from Jennifer? How do you let go of your false self and this story of who you are? Well, realize that you can't disconnect from something that doesn't exist. It's not really a disconnect, it's just realizing that you never existed, as what you thought you were.

It's recognizing that the mind has created this false filtered illusion over what's actually real. Trying to be a person completely blocks out what you truly are. And what exactly are you? Well labeling what you are is just another label. But you are Neter and Netert! You are Consciousness! You are Everything and Everyone. Yes, you are Everyone! How is that possible? Jennifer, so am I my mom and friend, Alecia? Well, mom and Alecia are just titles and labels.

They are also just characters of the mind. They truly don't exist.

You see, Jennifer is the one who believes in separation. It actually doesn't exist. Once you realize you don't exist, you'll realize nobody is actually here. Once you realize yourself for what you truly are you will clearly realize that you are everything.

Thus, you are beyond the body and mind. You are beyond personality. Now this does not mean to give up the Male and Female experience. Desires will still rise. You will still take care of what you need to take care of. You can still attract your dreams. There just won't be anyone here doing it, allowing you to be whatever you want. There will be nobody here to be afraid of or someone who is afraid.

You won't feel the need-to-need validation from others. Because others don't exist. We are all One! You won't feel this need to be someone for the world. You can just be! You will be Free to be. And don't try to paint a picture of what this experience would look like or be like. The mind cannot comprehend it nor can it create it or imagine it. You can only be this. You can only experience what I am pointing to. This will not be a conceptual knowing. Because, Jennifer, you cannot awaken to this. That's right, because Jennifer doesn't exist.

Thus, Jennifer asked, so does this mean Jennifer isn't the one aware? Correct!

It's awareness that's aware. It's consciousness realizing itself, not Jennifer realizing she is consciousness. So, to truly be Free from suffering, from trying to be someone for the world, from caring about how others perceive you, you must realize that you were never this person to begin with. One conscious being is more powerful than one billion unconscious beings, going against you.

Because you know that what you truly are, is Everything and Everyone. Look past the titles, names, labels, appearances, and self-pride and you will rediscover yourself.

Thus, what is a Person? What is it? Well, from reading and studying this chapter, do you still want or are you sure you still want to call yourself a Person? Hey, they change your originality from Neter and Netert, to a Person, to dumbing you down to their level.

Even if ones looking from the point of view from Ballentine's Law Dictionary, so-call 1948 Edition, Person is defined as: "Monster or Lower animal."

You are not a person, so stop trying to be one or letting someone call you a person. Reset your mind and heart and find out that you are an Expert in any subject using this chapter and book, period. Never forget that you are a Neter and Netert. And always remember that person, god, devil, human, human being, monster, barbarian, and lower animal is one and the same thing and cannot be awakened nor be aware either.

Chapter 5: You're Not a Human or Human Being

Hello, here is the power in realizing you are not a human or human being.

It's a guarantee that you are not going to view who you think you are the same way after reading this chapter for a while.

Now, I will lightweight ask you some questions and want you to act like we are having a conversation. So who are you? If you answered stating your names on your so-called birth certification you are incorrect. You are not names. So now who are you? Well to tell you the truth, pretty much any answer you give to me is incorrect. But if you were completely silent, though, you are actually pretty close to figuring it out.

Thus, we have grown to identify ourselves with ideas and beliefs and with our thoughts, and problems. If I also asked you to describe yourself, you would start talking about your age and where you grew up and what you do for a living.

But you are not those things. How could you be a name? How could you be a profession? How could you be your pain?

All of those things come and go and change.

And who you are truly cannot change or come and go. Who you are is always here and it's the same all the time.

Hence, let me explain it a little bit more so that you can comprehend better who you truly are. Let's say you suffer from what they called anxiety. Anxiety is when you are constantly anxious about the so-called future. Your mind creates all these assumptions and fake scenarios to keep you stuck in your room away from expressing yourself fully. So, who is the one aware of this happening? You are the awareness of your anxiety. You are not anxiety. And the one aware cannot be the one suffering. Because you're also the one aware of the suffering happening. But note, remember though it's not you who is even suffering. Even suffering is an illusion. Because it's the mind that creates it. It's not real!

However more, this applies to everything.

When you are overthinking, who is aware of this happening? So now, before this chapter ends, I want you to really experience who you truly are. I want you to realize that you are not your pain and suffering and that you're not even human at a deeper level. You are about to experience what it's like to return to your true nature. So now notice how you are aware of your human character reading this chapter and book. Become aware of this experience, no thoughts are needed to be aware. If thoughts rise notice how you are the awareness of those also. You're not a human becoming aware of a human.

You are above human. Yes, you are so much more. Now become aware again of any little noise in the background. Just listen it. Don't judge it. Don't think about it. Just experience what it's like to listen. Now that you have a sense of being aware, to come aware of your awareness, don't focus on any experience, focus on the awareness itself. You cannot experience this or comprehend this medley. So stop thinking about how to do it, you are not your thoughts. Become aware of something and then become aware of the sense of awareness and just stay there for a moment. Keep returning back to it every time you fall back into thought.

Thus, whenever you are suffering you can just ask your nature who is aware of this happening.

But don't answer it mentally. Just go directly into becoming aware of awareness. This is who you really are. You are not the sad story of your so-called life. You are not your so called past and mistakes. You are pure consciousness awareness. Any problem you have is only there because you are aware of it. But it's not who you are. Who you truly are cannot be affected by anything.

Because you are the observer of it. And no, doing this will not cause you to start dissociating. This is literally you reverting back to your natural state of pure love, peace, joy and confidence. Sitting and becoming aware of your awareness will liberate you from all suffering. Because you will begin to realize that the suffering has nothing to do with you.

You will start detaching from those limiting beliefs. It will be so easy and effortless to let go of things. You are Life itself. You are the Present moment. You are a Neter and Netert!

Hence, the power within us is very, very powerful. And words cannot even explain the experience of reverting back to it. One thing you need to know is to fully comprehend that you can improve your human character that they brainwashed and miseducated you to be, and become whoever you truly want to be in this lifetime. Once you realize who you truly are there is nothing that can stop you from getting what you want in life. You can change because you are not your factitious system.

29

Because you can improve it. You are not the story of your life. Because you can improve it, too. You are not your depression and anxiety. Because you are aware of it and can definitely improve it. If you believe you cannot, well that's just a factitious mindset, and you can improve that too.

However, everyone is literally the same. We just have different beliefs and perspectives that create a unique nature. You are the creator of your reality. All of this was created just for you, to create whatever you want.

But you have been blinded. So make a Choice and take the consciousness medicine and rediscover the truth about your nature, so that you can take your Power back.

Thus, so just remember whenever you find your nature struggling mentally or whatever it may be, notice what you are, the awareness of it, and then go deeper and become aware of the awareness, and just focus on that. Let go of the outside experience and just look at awareness. Just look at your consciousness.

Now, so if I were to ask you who are you now, how would you reply?

My answer would be, you are a Neter and Netert. And I wish that would be your answer too.

Because from reading above you can truly comprehended that you are not a human or human being. Are you sure now you want to call yourself a Human or Human being? From Ballentine's Law Dictionary, [so-called 1948] Edition. "Human being is defined as follows: See monster, from the same dictionary, monster is defined: "A human being by birth, but in some part resembling a lower animal."

Thus only Neter and Netert knows that they have so much word spell on you that you would not even can comprehend that the word: human, human being, God, person, devil, monster, barbarian, savage, Satan, and lower animal, are one and the same word and mean the same thing. Whosoever, call or name or label themselves as these words cannot be enlightened, awaken, or can't come into awareness or consciousness. They have to stay in the nature of that word, because as you all know that a leopard cannot change its spots.

Thus, to show you that God and Person is the same word we shall look no further than in the Signs and Symbols of Primordial Man, by Albert Churchward, who wrote: "The conclusion that these old Priests arrived at in their Eschatology--"That God is a Person," ...

Now how did their own Ballentine Law Dictionary define the word person again? "Monster or lower animal."

You are a Neter and Netert! That's what you should know and start to represent as a Neter and Netert, not as a human or human being or person. There is a POWER in Realizing you are not a Human!

Chapter 6: You're Not the Doer of Life, Free Will is an Illusion

Here comes this chapter, you have to vide this to really realize what I am going to say or saying. Thinking about what I am about to talk and write about can be very difficult to comprehend. So if I told you hey, you have never done anything and you are not in control at all. You would hit me and say well since I am not in control, I guess I didn't do that. And I would agree. Because like I said you have never done anything. During my Divine Wisdom journey, before my enlightenment realization, right before I began having these transformational rediscover shifts, I was really into the teachings of non-duality and astrology.

I feel like once you're seeking energy leads you to those teachings, it's when things really start changing. It was the beginning of my Consciousness and the end of my unconsciousness. Non-duality and Astrology will teach you that who you always believed your nature to be never existed. And those teachings will bring you to the realization of Oneness. Well at least that's how it was for me. Through these teachings you come across some things that would come off crazy if you had no idea what this journey of Divine Wisdom is about.

Thus, things such as you don't exist. You don't have a life. You don't have free will. You aren't and have never done anything. And things like nobody is actually here. This completely goes against the reality of the mind. The reality that most of us have grown into believing to be what's real. But as you become curious and as you begin going within and sitting in silence with your own nature, these things began to no longer become beliefs.

You start to actually seeing and experiencing these things to be true. You know them. And it has nothing to do with beliefs and concepts.

Thus, you began to see how useless beliefs are, when it comes to the Divine Wisdom journey. Because the shifts that you seek for, cannot happen through an conceptual Knowing. It's all energetically realized.

You have to experience the truth, not believe in it. Please don't believe anything I am saying. See it to be true!

Thus, when I come across the saying you aren't doing anything, you aren't the doer of life. It honestly was one of the biggest shifts I had for self-realization. Therefore, please see if you can realize what I am pointing to for the rest of this chapter. This can help you with self-realization tremendously. Hence, let's chat about meditation first.

You can participate and see this to be true for your nature, if you would like to right now. Just close your eyes and be. So many of us struggle with meditation and it's because we think it's an activity. We think meditation is something we do, and that's why it appears to be difficult, because we are trying to be in control. Thus, you may try to stop thoughts or try whatsoever you're trying to do. But meditation isn't a doing.

It's just something that is happening along with everything else. Everything! Nobody is doing anything because nobody here. Things are just happening. And meditation is one of the best ways to realize this. Even though it feels like you are in control. You are not!

However, when I say you, I'm talking about who you believe your nature to be. If your name is Jade, Jade isn't sitting down to meditate. Jade isn't doing a guided meditation, because Jade doesn't actually exist. Jade you are just an idea, you are a creation of the mind. A self-pride creation.

Thus, if you realize what you truly are as Neter and Netert, as awareness, as consciousness from that seed of pure being. You will realize that awareness isn't involved in activity. It's just aware of what's happening, and you are this awareness. You better notice this! Even if your self-pride is bringing up its beliefs, and it's trying to counter what I am pointing to, the self-pride can agree that awareness is just aware, not affected by anything because it has no form. You can't do anything to awareness. Awareness cannot do anything because it's just aware. If you can realize that things are just happening meditation becomes effortless and that's because meditation is the release of effort, the release of trying, you will realize there is just a vessel, a body and mind within me. Me as in awareness! It's not my body, it's not my mind, because awareness is just awareness.

It's not an issue with your own nature. There is nobody here to claim to have anything. Thus, now we can go back to the illusion of control and the illusion of the doer. Ask your nature who's the one reading this chapter? Who's the one doing the activity of reading this chapter? Did you just say your name or me? Well, where does this someone you believe your nature to be exist? Did you look at your body or say here? Well, where in the body does this someone exist? What part of the body are you if you are the body?

The Chest? The heart? The head? Notice that whatever or wherever you think you exist, it's just a sensation that you are labeling me or you. Without the mind you're just aware of energy of a sensation.

The mind is the father of lies. You cannot find who you believe your nature to be.

Jade you only exist within the mind...

You are awareness. It's what we are as One. We don't have individual awareness.

We have individual experiences. Awareness is just awareness. Realize how within you every experience happens. Everything happens within you. You aren't doing anything. It's all just happening. We aren't human doings. We are Neter and Netert. Some of you might question me, well if I'm not in control, how could you manifest and create your own existence or naturality? It's all just happening.

Thus, manifesting is happening. Those desires that arise to create something, it just happens. Thoughts you don't think them! They just arise. They just happen. Actions we don't do them. They just happen. Many will also say, well I can go an kill about 1000 of us and just say I didn't do it. Yes it's true, you as what you truly are didn't do anything. But that doesn't mean consequences shouldn't be given, but not by the illusion of man-made law. You're completely lost your mind if you think that. Those actions happen because we are unconscious of our consciousness.

So teach them consciousness and not punishment. You're completely locked in with the self-pride. It's honestly like you are possessed. We all were or are possessed by the self-prize. And some self-pride or so strong that they completely keep you close minded, to finding out that you are Neter and Netert. Hence, what you are is Life itself. What you are is control. You are the energy that animates life. Things only happen because of you. Nothing can happen without you. If there is an experience, then there is you.

It's like playing play station or any game where you are controlling the characters. Ok now let's say this character in the game is who you believe your nature to be. You have completely forgotten that you are the one outside of the game controlling it. So everything that's being done within the game, you have the sense of I am doing this, I am the character in this game doing things and I have full control over my life. Thus, this is the delusion that the self-pride has trapped you into believing. Because it feels real. Because it feels like you are the thinker of thoughts and you are the body. That's what you believe and you so convinced of it too.

The characters in the game are completely unconscious.

They have no idea that there is someone or something outside of the game controlling everything. They have No idea!

And they for sure don't realize that it's what they truly are. Now I ask you to just apply that to this experience. See life as a game.

I mean it truly is like a game or a dream.

And know that you are not the character in this game. You're just experiencing one.

You're just aware of one. Do you feel pain?

No! The body does, and you are aware of it. You are experiencing it. Do you think thoughts?

No! Thoughts arise and you are just effortlessly aware of it. Do you do things? No!

Things happen and you are just aware of it.

Thus, stop trying to control life. You trying to control life cause resistance. Let life flow!

Life is trying to flow through you, and you keep blocking it, by trying to control something you can't control. Even you trying to control is also something that's just happening. I know how it can get confusing. It can be hard to find the correct words or saying to explain something unexplainable.

Hence, I wish you're beginning to realize this all. It's very hilarious actually when you realize it. Also very freeing and peaceful. Now remember the mind cannot be used to transcend the mind. Go above it, observe it, without attachment and identity. The mind cannot awaken.

Jade cannot awaken. Consciousness will realize its consciousness. Sit in the reality outside of the mind and you will realize your true nature to be everything. There you have it, well said.

However, do you remember earlier on in this Chapter I mentioned that free will is an illusion?

Well let me clear this free will illusion up so we all can be free from this illusion. However, free will is a pretty difficult or tedious subject to debate upon. Because many of us still have this sense of me. This sense of I am doing this or making that decision. But only to recognize that there is no self. We believe that I am making this decision and that I am in full control, is real. But are you really making decisions and in control? Free will is the ability to make your own decisions and to have that ownership over the actions you take. Thus laws in every country take your free will and ownership from you. However, once again there is no you. I will try my ought most best to explain this to make it possible for you. You don't have to take my word for it though.

Thus, I want you to experiment with this, to see this to be true for your own nature. Free will does not exist, in the first place. Yes, there is a will but it is not free though. For example:

you did not choose to go pick this book up. Even though it may feel like it was you whom made this decision, it wasn't. The brain and body are constantly active. There was an impulse to go to the bookstore or library to pick this book up and then a decision was made in the brain to read this chapter and the whole book, and it all happened without the idea of you. Things are just happening.

Hence, decisions are being made so fast and automatically we attach this false self to the decision as if it was us who made the decision.

But that's not true. Because first there is no one here to make decisions. Decisions aren't happening to anyone, they are just happening. I know it may sound crazy and confusing all in one. I also didn't want to believe this to be true, but as I inquired this in my own experience, I constantly seen that I never had control. I never had control over my thoughts. Because thoughts are just happening, and they are happening to no one. I never had control over my decisions. Because decisions are just happening, and they are happening to no one.

Hence, if you are not familiar with the true and correct non-dual teachings or the true and correct teachings of consciousness, please get familiar with it all. When I say it's happening to no one, you may think I am insane, so I'll give you a quick explanation to what I mean.

To get straight to the point, you don't exist! No body exists. Well, we exist but not as these so-called human, characters.

Nobody= No-body, Nothing = No-thing.

However, comprehend that you cannot find yourself in the body. I said, go ahead and try. You don't exist behind the eyes. You don't exist in the chest or in the head. That sense of self that you are identifying with us is just a sensation. It's just energy and this energy is boundless. It is no edge, you cannot find the edge of a sensation, it goes on and on and out forever, beyond the body. These sensations also have no density. It may feel solid but it's just energy vibrating. Solids do not exist. If you go deep into a solid, all you will find is empty space. It can appear to be solid but there is no such thing. The Universe and everything in it is created up of 99. 9 percent empty space.

Thus, nothing is actually what it appears to be. So, if you don't exist what are you? Well, me and you and everything around you are pure consciousness. There is no self. There is no doer.

There is no thinker. There is no listener. There is no one here suffering. Everything is just happening. No one is feeling. No one is talking. No one is reading this book. There is no one here. All of this is just happening, and it's happening to no one. Now, you tell me how would there be free will, if things are just happening? Do you clearly comprehend what I am saying? I know it feels very real. But right now, you may be disagreeing, but you are only disagreeing because you still have that sense of self. That sense of me doing something. And to be truth with you, I am not expecting you to not feel that way. But it's all an illusory sense. Because this self that you believe yourself to be has never existed.

Hence, have you ever been traveling and you get caught up in thoughts or even stop paying attention to traveling, but somehow you still know where to go, you still know how to stay on the road. You still can follow all of the road requirements and then you snap back and realize that you weren't even paying close attention to traveling. But traveling was just happening without the idea of you or even the focus on the activity. Traveling was just happening without you thinking you were in control. Are you breathing, are you pumping your blood throughout your body, are you digesting food, are you thinking, or is all of this just happening and rising from nowhere? It's all just happening.

Thus, any sounds you hear are just happening and they are rising from nothingness. There isn't even a left or a right, or an up or a down. These sounds are coming out of nowhere, and there is no one here listening.

It's just happening. You aren't choosing to listen to something. Whatever is happening in your experience is just happening. It's hard to put this into words. Comprehend that my words are not the truth. They are simply to point you to it. Me not saying anything and being silent, is closer to the truth than me speaking. Please throughout your day stop and just notice how you actually aren't doing anything, and things are just happening.

Try this.

Lift your foot up right now.

So, did you look at your foot? Did you begin turning and observing your foot or did you simply just raise your foot while still focusing on the book or did you not participate in that at all? Regardless of what happened, it just happened. And I know it feels like it was you who chose to do so. But it just happened. A decision was made in the brain without the idea of you and what we truly are, was simply just aware of the decision and the action.

It's pretty liberating for me to know that I don't have the control that I think I have. Think about animals. Do you think they have free will? Do you think they have thoughts about what to do next and this sense of control? No, they don't!

They are simply letting life guide them. It's amazing how animals don't need instructions on how to live. They're just letting intuition take control. They are letting life take care of life. They have no control and neither do we. Things are just happening.

However, you may say well what if I want to go to a Vegan Restaurant, I'm clearly choosing to eat at this vegan Restaurant? No, no, you are not choosing that. Hunger rises in the body and decisions on where to eat rise also. And then the brain also chooses what decision to go with, based on your desires and preferences. And this all happens without the idea of a nature. And now eating a tantalizing delicious vegan meal is happening. It's all just happening and it's happening to no one.

It would be my pleasure to write more books on subjects like this one, because it can be very tedious to comprehend mentally. It's a lot more clear to see through experience though. Nevertheless, just try to see that you have no control. It will help you realize this more than these words can say. I don't want you to believe me. I want you to see this to be true for your nature.

And that applies to every single thing that you see or heard me write and talk about. Try to see this in your experience. And this the bottom line, know that free will does not exist.

Chapter 7: You Are Neter and Netert, The Grafted Essence is the Devil

Distinguishably, I have come to my consciousness to aware that all instruction is either about things or about signs, symbols, names, titles and labels; but things are learnt by means of signs, symbols, names, titles and labels. Here I use the word "thing" in a strict sense to signify or symbolize that which is never employed as a sign or symbol of anything else, for example, God, Devil, stone, cattle, wood and other things of that kind. Hence, it is these same signs, symbols, instructions, names, titles, labels, and things they are using to so-called control you and your mind, and in their word what they called reality.

To say now that the word God and Devil is a sign and symbol, instruction, name, title and label. The ancient Neter and Netert have no clue what the word God mean, and they never heard of such word, but they know and heard of the word Neter and Netert, because Nordic Devils graft the word God from the word Neter and derive the word Goddess from the word Netert. Now are you one who prefers the last comers to the first comers? The moral is everywhere misanthropic and antisocial. Now to show you that you are Neter and Netert, and the grafted Essence is the Devil, I have to explain the word Neter and Netert, God and Devil, Heaven and hell and soul to you all.

44

Now we have historically and traditionally, brainwashed and mis-educated, and mis-leaded and indoctrinated and ideologically have the word hell explained and portrayed as this place of everlasting suffering. It's said to be the location in the afterlife where <u>souls</u> go to suffer and to be tortured. A place where they can never escape once they are there, and the ruler of the realm is known as <u>Satan </u>or the <u>Devil</u>. However, now, <u>heaven</u> is said to be this place of pure, love, light and joy, where suffering does not exist, and the ruler of <u>heaven</u> is <u>God</u>, the one and only creator.

Thus, before I began the explaining my nature, I want to say I like Diocletian, have no respect for no religions and no religious walks of life.

This chapter is written to destroy all religions and religious head strong. I used to be a religious one too, but since my awakening my facts and eyes have opened to something new. So try your best to see where I am coming from. So with that being said about hell and heaven and God and the Devil and the soul and Satan, what if these stories were meant to be taking literal. Well don't let me burst your bubble, because the word hell is the Alkebulan word for the Sun. So that hell story is a lie! Remember that the first or original Alkebulan Neter and Netert is the only one who have souls, and as scientist say Nordic Devil family don't have souls. As you can see this is backed by science.

If you don't have soul, you have got to be the Devil, then? In ancient Alkebulan heaven is the state of mind or state of condition. That's prove their heaven story to be a lie also.

45

Refresh your mind of Chapter four and Chapter 5 of this book where I point out that God, Person, Devil, Human being, Human, Satan, Savage, Barbarian etc. etc., are one and the same thing and in meaning, too.

Hence, I truly believe that the Torah, Bible, Qur'an or Koran and all religions in general has been portrayed and force upon us who never research and study them. Because every religion is talking about you when they speak of Supreme Being, and that evil force they speak of is the Grafted Essence. Let's break this down.

Just take a moment to hear me out Neter and Netert!

Anything is grafted is the sign and symbol of the Devil. God is grafted from the Alkebulan word, Neter. If you don't believe me, go and study the Egyptian Book of the Dead (The Papyri's of Ani) Egyptian Text Transliteration and Translation, edited by E. A. Wallis Budge; and An Egyptian Hieroglyphic Dictionary Vol 1 and 2, edited by E.A. Wallis Budge. Neter and Netert is Consciousness, the Creator, the Protector, the Observer, the All Knowing of everything and so are we.

Thus, you see there is only one consciousness, because consciousness has no form. You cannot locate consciousness, no matter how hard you search for it. These bodies, these vessels that we can control is not who we are, I tell you Neter and Netert.

You created this body. These bodies are just a way of consciousness expressing its nature. Notice how your body is created within consciousness. It's not the other way around. These are just objects that we are aware of. Can you agree with me on this, that you are aware of your body? Notice the difference in saying I am the body, and I am aware of the body. There is a very different sense to both of those statements. And just to let you know that you cannot be what you are aware of. Because you are the awareness of it. No experience or object can be you. Because you are the awareness of it.

Now if you were to directly connect with your consciousness by becoming aware of your awareness or should I say awakening to who you truly are, you will begin to notice that the one who is aware isn't affected by any experience that may be present. Regardless if it's your thoughts or feelings or a life situation, the one who is aware is simply just aware, and the one who is aware is just at peace.

Thus, it's present, it's not suffering, it's accepting, it's always been here in the background, it's limitless and boundless. It's the place where suffering cannot exist.

It's Neter and Netert presence! It's your true Being. All of these teachings that tell you to follow a Supreme Being and trust in a Supreme Being it's supposed to point to you awakening to realizing that this Neter and Netert is you. Neter and Netert isn't outside of you, it's who we all truly are. We share the exact same Being as Neter and Netert, because there is only one Being. You and I are the same. You are the honeybees and birds. You are nature and the trees. You are the bugs, ants, cows and lions that roam the earth and air. You are this Neter and Netert. And many will say well if I was Neter and Netert why can't I do this and do that.

Because we are Neter and Netert having a Male and Female body experience. The same way dogs and goats are Neter and Netert have a dog and goat body experience. Yes, you are your dogs and goats. Don't the Air always connect us? You are everything! And this is very difficult for some of us to accept, because of what we all have been taught, and I completely comprehend and respect that. But I will try my best to get you to see where I am coming from. Hence, I will now get back to how we are Neter and Netert. But let's move on to how the Devil is just the grafted essence. Remember how I said once, you can just be present and become aware of who you truly are? You will see that suffering doesn't exist there, well to be truthful suffering doesn't exist where Neter and Netert exists, because the grafted essence cannot exist there. Thoughts cannot exist or damage you in the present moment, if you are thinking you are not fully present. The grafted essence doesn't exist there. Suffering can only exist within the mind through thoughts.

If you are suffering it is because of the grafted essence around you. It is because of the devil! Hell is the name of the sun in the Alkebulan language, and it is just a state of mind in the English word meaning, and once you are trapped in it your life will feel like you are suffering. I know you all have heard of some of these before. The Devil is the one that tells you that you are not enough, that you aren't worthy. It's what makes you worry and have anxiety, it's where regret and depression exist, it's where fear exists. It's the very first thing telling you that this book is BS and has no truth in it.

The grafted essence doesn't want to die and wants to stay in full control. That sounds familiar, right? The Devil doesn't want you to realize who you truly are, because it knows it will die once you awaken. Love is all you need. The Devil will no longer have control over your life.

Hence, the Ancient Alkebulan Neter and Netert well known Supreme Being that is a part of Divine wisdom, didn't know or heard of religion or religious beings. Alkebulan Ancient Neter and Netert didn't believe they were separated from other Neter and Netert. They knew that they were Neter and Netert. The only Divine book we have is the Book of coming Forth by Day, commonly known as the Egyptian Book of the Dead, edited by E.A. Wallis Budge, which referred to Alkebulan as Neter and Netert. They travel around the earth trying to tell others that they and all other Alkebulans were Neter and Netert and they must remain that way, and the grafted essence hated them and betrayed them for speaking and teaching the truth and no matter what others said they knew this to be true.

Because the Ancient Alkebulan Neter and Netert were awakened to their true Supreme Being. They were conscious of their consciousness. While everyone around them was unconscious. Just like in this present moment.

Thus, there is no difference if you look good, bet- ween you and our Ancient Alkebulan Neter and Netert.

49

Because we are all One. There is only one Being, and it's Neter and Netert, Being. And it's who we truly are.

Forget about all those names, titles and labels that they give us on some so-called birth certificate, to divide and separate and lead us into unconsciousness from our one and only name, Neter and Netert. You are everyone who has ever lived and deceased, and you will be everyone who has yet to come upon this earth. I'll give you an example of how sharp Ancient Alkebulan Neter and Netert were of this knowing. The story of Asar's body has been cut up and spread all over, and Ast went looking for his body parts and putting them back together is traumatic. But even though those who did it know why they did it, Asar and Ast still loved them.

Asar and Ast are Neter and Netert, and Neter and Netert know that whoever calls themselves God, Devil, person, human, human being, monster, barbarian, savage and lower animal are unconscious, so they forgive them of their envious self.

Hence, their behavior and actions came from their grafted essence. From the Devil nature.

From an unconscious state. Do you think if these Devils were awakened and conscious of who they truly are, they would have still done what they have done? Yes, they would! The same behavior of them still takes place at this present, in all society that they live in throughout the earth by these Devils. If you walked around telling everyone that we are Neter and Netert, and we are all connected, they will look at you like your crazy. But that's only because they are unconscious, for this truth. And also, because they are still slaves to the Devil mind. We can all experience what they called heaven, right on this Earth. Hell and heaven aren't a realm in the afterlife. They exist here.

If you are trapped inside the mind you will perish. If you are present and free from the mind and all the false identifications, you will experience the true state or condition of heaven. However, heaven is explained to be a place of peace and love and happiness. Well, once you are awakened to who you truly are, you will notice that you have been this peace, love and happiness that you have been seeking for your whole life, all along. You are the All-Knowing. The Essence of who you are is who Neter and Netert is. You are the Source. You are the Universe.

You are what lies behind all comprehending. Neter and Netert is the Creator and so are you. Now just picture how this green Planet Earth would be at present if everyone was awakened to this knowledge or have been taught this knowledge in schools, colleges and their universities. The Earth would be at peace, and flow happiness everywhere. Love would flow through the air.

However, I want you to know that I do not know everything. So there may be some holes in my knowledge. But I wish you were able to see what I bring to the knowledge table.

My intentions are pure and positive, with every Knowledge. So I wish this knowledge was able to at least strike some sense of curiosity in you all who read this book or heard of this book. I deal with facts and truth, you can come with your "A" game of opinions.

Thus, if any of you want to experience that true state or condition of heaven, transcendental meditation will tremendously take you there. Self-inquiry will make you realize your true nature, and that you are Neter and Netert. And non-duality will eventually prove to you that we are all One. And that we are all connected. You are Neter and Netert, the grafted Nordic Devil essence is the Devil.

Even though that we are all connected I am going to show you who are Neter and Netert and who are the Devil, and how the Devil comes about and how nothing cannot change we Neter and Netert. For example, just remember that the only proof they have to show that spiderman exists is the spiderman comic books. But at present we have living proof of Neter and Netert and the Devil still living and alive. I shall refute all scientists, hermogenes, prophets, prophetess and messengers.

Thus, you are Neter and Netert. Neter and Netert is the first word. Neter and Netert is First. Neter and Netert is One. Neter and Netert is Original.

Now, if Neter and Netert is One, it must necessarily be a unique property that it may belong to One. What will be unique and singular, if not that to which nothing equal can be produced? What will be principal, if not that which is above all things and before all things and from which all things have originated? It is by having these qualities alone that Neter and

Netert is Neter and Netert, and by having them alone, that Neter and Netert is One. If another being should possess them as well, then there will be as many Neter and Netert as there are beings which possess the qualities proper to Neter and Netert.

Hence, it is that Scientists and Hermogenes misled and try to bring in two Neter and Netert-- they introduce grafted essence as equal to Neter and Netert. But Neter and Netert must be One, because that is Neter and Netert which is Supreme; but nothing can be unique if something can be put on a level with it; but grafted essence will be put on a par with Neter and Netert, when it is authoritatively declared to be eternal. Thus I said to you over and over that the word God and Goddess are Germanic/ Dutch words that they grafted from the Alkebulan word Neter and Netert.

Have a look in the Book of Coming forth by Day [commonly known as] The Egyptian Book of The Dead, edited by E.A. Wallis Budge. The word God and Goddess could never be equal to the word Neter and Netert that it is grafted from. We Alkebulans are the Neter and Netert. Everything is grafted from us.

Thus, any live germ grafted from the original is devil. In grafted a life from a life that is original, that which we graft from the original, regardless to what life it is, it is weaker than that which it was grafted from. We are reducing the power of that original when we graft from it. When we graft fruit, the fruit that we graft is not the equal to that which we graft it out of. And so it is when it comes to life, whether it's birds, whether it's a beast, animals, or a man. Now you see what the grafted word God is?

Northwestern Asia, Nordic devil family is a grafted family that is made and diagnosed with two main genetic disease conditions, to prove they are grafted and the Devil. One is Albinism, in which they lack the Melanin Pigment that makes their skin, nose and hair extremely pale and straight, and the other is Heterochromia, in which their eyes are different in colour. That is how you know the Devil! Please, say No to these Devil qualities!

Thus, they can never say their word God and Goddess are equal to Neter and Netert and they can never say they are equal to us Neter and Netert. They are a part of us because they are grafted from us, but they are not us, Neter and Netert. You might have known, but many already know that for centuries that you can graft animals, the Original Neter and Netert, plants, and fruits for desired qualities or purposes.

This is exactly how the story of Asar otherwise Neter goes, how they cut or otherwise graft Neter up to their so-called: Black man or Negro or African man, White man the European, yellow man the Chinese man, brown man the Indian man or Arab man or Spanish man, Jenifer Foster, or Jade Scott, Ayon Skyers, Dave Smith, Roy Jones, Alecia Johnson, Paul Williams, Jack Blake, John Clarke, Tasha Brown, Faye Harts etc., etc..

And the cut up or grafting of the One Original Neter continues just like that where none of us realize that we all name Neter and Netert, which is Protector, Creator, Everything and Everyone and Unity.

Now they can have all of those cut up and grafted divisions, plus they also can have the myth of chosen people, native, indigenous, and nationality. But me and all other Neter and Netert will claim First or Original, Or One or Neter and Netert. The greatest and the highest of all titles and names, and labels and positions.

You and I are Neter and Netert and those with the genetic disease of Albinism and Heterochromia are the grafted Nordic Devil. Those intellectual know it all who use the word God, but now ask those same intellectual who know it all who used the term God, who and what is God or what God looks like? If they cannot define God or something in detail and they just blow you off or shun you off, they are a fraud. So, I turned to one of their smartest websites called Cleverbot.com and I asked: who and what is God? And it answered and said, "The Creator of the Universe." So, I then ask, what does God looks like then, since you said God is the Creator of the Universe? It said to me, "I don't know, do you?" Now, you see the fraud?

Hence, I will define and give you the meaning of the Germanic/Dutch word God as follow. In the book called Signs and Symbols, edited by Albert Churchward he wrote: "The conclusion that these old Priests arrived at in their Eschatology – "That God is a Person" ...

Now the Black's Law Dictionary define the word:

Person, as: "human or human being." However, the Ballentine's Law Dictionary defines the word: human or human being, as: "Monster or lower: animal." So the word: God, Person, Human, Human being, Monster, Devil, Barbarian, savage and low animal are one and the same word and meaning. So why would you call yourself one of these words? You are Neter and Netert and nothing else!

Now remember this. You cannot be Neter and Netert and God or Devil or Man or Woman, or King or Queen or President, or Prime Minister or Judge or Scientist, or Doctor, Governor or Mayor or Prosecutor or lawyer or Police officer or soldier etc., etc., at the same time. It's impossible!

As a Neter and Netert you are Original and Natural to every bit of this Cosmos. The Webster's II New College Dictionary, Third Edition, 2005, by Houghton Mifflin Company, page 1242, gives the meaning and definition and identity of you when it gives the mean of: Uraeus, as: "The figure of the Sacred Serpent, depicted on the headdress of ancient Egyptian Ruler and Deities as an emblem of Sovereignty." In support, the Greek historian- Herodotus, who learned history and other disciplines from the indigenous Africans of Egypt from 450 B.C.E., described them in his Histories, Book II, in the Following way: "The Egyptians, Colchians, and Ethiopians have thick lips, broad noses, woolly hair, and they are burnt of skin."

Herodotus description fit I Ayon Skyers and any "Negro" in the Harlem's of the United States of America and elsewhere over and on this Cosmos. Give honor to Yosef Ben Jochannan, in support of your true identity! Neter is Male, and Netert is Female!

Chapter 8: You Are the Creator

One thing I must surely do is to make it clear that you are the true Creator and the true source of your own reality. The Cosmos is not outside of you. Look within your nature. Everything that you want you already are and have. To prove that you are the true Creator and true source of your own reality go and read James Hastings book called: Encyclopedia of Religion and Ethics vol-1-13, and you will see where he points out all the Grand Universities and Grand Khuti that we built all over this Cosmos. And we have made the Nordic devil family out of us Neter and Netert, to show how great our destiny is. That we created what we want instead of begging for it today. What a low-down dirty shame this is upon us today.

Hence, most of us lack the awareness that we actively determine our own existence. We simply accept circumstances and events as they present to us. Allowing these occurrences to shape our way of life as the Nordic devil family wants it to be. The notion that our ancient knowledge can exclusively determine our being is embraced without acknowledging our capacity to consciously craft our own knowledge.

This eye-opening awareness serves as a simple reminder. You are the Creator for your own reality. Over the course of ages so-called intellectual giants' theories have discussed an alleged Big Bang theory an instance in which all energy and matter existed within an infinitesimal point. Only to erupt and give rise to the vast Cosmos.

This Big Bang theory phenomenon is synonymous with the consciousness presently engaged. You are in existence, the same expansive Big Bang theory that has traversed the cosmos for an immeasurable span of countless ages.

Thus, within you resides wisdom that encompasses all other knowledge. You are seamlessly intertwined with and as the Creator and the universal source.

You have always been Neter and Netert!

But to fully experience the range of life you had to become a little trap within the limits of the Nordic devil family way of life. You had to take on the Devil society in this Cosmos with all its doubts and uncertainties. But even in that state you are still part of the body of peace and love, and tranquility existed with the origin of the cosmos. The challenge lies in the forgotten awareness of your true nature.

At present we falter and begin perceiving our nature as vulnerable beings subject to the mercy of circumstances. We were never taught that we have the power to create the reality we want. As I show in the beginning of this chapter. The critical aspect however is not the mechanics of creation, but rather the ongoing act of creation revealing in the present moment as thoughts and emotions and sensations stir while this knowledge exposes, they generate continuous frequencies. These frequencies send direct knowledge to the cosmos, akin to transmissions and visualize your brain and body as transmitters and emitters of these frequencies.

Thus, the persistent thoughts and feelings you generate serve as a Creator, creating and infusing the reality you experience. Your thoughts hold a powerful role in shaping reality.

They emit vibrations that affect various planes of existence. The vibrational frequency of your thought guides how they materialize in the Cosmos. So now, reality is shaped by both the external and internal cosmos. However, the latter can be accessed and protected through to movement of your own observation and thinking.

These ideas are grounded in the idea of the paradox where everything that exists is both real and unreal at the same instant. The Cosmos appears very real to us, but we must remember that we exist within the inner cosmos where everything is finite and limited. The Neter and Netert, and the Nordic devil and energies around us are real, real but in a deeper sense. They are simply part of our own consciousness awareness. The mind of Neter and Netert can be compared to a very beautiful garden which can be knowledgeable cultivated or left hidden and be filled with thorn bushes, but whether it is cultivated or neglected it is destined to produce. But yet if useful trees are not plant, then trees of destruction planted, will fall and grow abundantly and reproduce just as a farmer tends to his or her crop, keep it free from weeds cultivating the foods and vegetable it needs.

So must Neter and Netert also tend to the garden of his and her mind and heart.

Thus, clearing it of harmful, useless and impure thoughts and cultivating to perfection the foods and vegetables of correct useful and pure thoughts. These profound insights are inspired by our ancient Neter and Netert. Only by consciousness this process does a Neter and Netert eventually rediscover that He or She is the Neter and Netert of His or her Being, and the director of His and Her life. He and she also rediscover within their nature the creation of thought and comes to comprehend with increasing precision how the Higher power of thoughts and the elements of the mind operate in shaping His and Her Being circumstances and destiny. Despite this, Neter and Netert can interpret events through various lenses.

Thus, before acknowledging your capacity to continuously create reality, recognize your Higher power to choose perspective. Events aren't inherently positive or negative. They simply exist. It's simply a fact from an energy source. Things simply are. You are the one who defines if circumstances are positive or negative. If things are correct or incorrect. But the main query remains: on what basis? By what means have you formed these perceptions?

However, comprehending your higher power to choose, how to perceive reality is of utmost importance. This underscores the importance of doubt and belief questioning what's presented and upholding your own common sense.

A sense that goes beyond dogmas and preconceived ideas. It's simply about authentically being your nature, shedding the weight of information that has been forced upon you. We need to put our knowledge into action, so that it becomes a part of our experiences and not just theoretical information. By doing so we can fully comprehend the depth of the knowledge of thought and how it can be used to shape our wellbeing, back to the origin of Neter and Netert and Creator.

Hence, knowledge is only great and valuable when it is put into action. Your own experiences are unique. They hold your true wisdom. While knowledge at present makes some of us think they are better than others, causing doubts and arguments about what is truth and what is untruth. It's the realm of action and experience that holds the essence of truth.

Action and experience are real, true and inherently perfect. Rediscovering your consciousness of your true nature beyond the clutter of force information is key. Acknowledge your potential and greatness equal to that of any revered Neter and Netert you admire. You possess the same mind, body and capacity to create, perceive and feel. The make-up lies in how you handle transmitted information, and what you absorb from the Cosmos, from reality.

Thus, consider a simple experiment. Say the Scenario where we went fishing on a boat and everyone on the boat collectively conveyed to a Netert that she appeared quite unwell.

Everyone in this setting agrees to participate.

As the fishing trip goes, those on the boat repeatedly communicated that she seemed sick. Initially she treated it as a joke. But with continuous repetition something peculiar occurred. Gradually she began to genuinely feel unwell, experiencing dizziness and severe chest pains. Eventually, she even came to think that she was genuinely ill. In the end, she was informed that this was just an experiment.

Hence, this scenario highlights how embracing something as true can profoundly shape the reality of one's experiences. Similar to this, Neter and Netert dealing with such circumstances, you too encounter countless perspectives on reality each day. This is why, in the very moment and through this, this dedicated book was meant for you.

I welcome you sincerely to question your true nature. To give more importance to what you feel and think, than to what others say.

However, this pertains especially to the capacities and abilities you hold within. Embrace your latent potential. The only limits are those nature imposed. There are no limits except the one that you have created your nature.

It is the moment to wake up. It is the moment to remember the wonder of who you are. It is the moment to expand that wonderful light, that creativity and that unlimited love and peace that you are, that is within you.

It is the moment to know what is Eschatology and Theology. Eschatology vs. Theology.

Thus, Eschatology is what our ancient Neter and Netert knows and teaches. They have no clue what is theology. Eschatology is created along with us Neter and Netert, and teaches about Neter and Netert, and that we are the Creator. While theology is man-made, totally grafted by the Nordic devil family to brainwash you with a Germanic/ Dutch word called God. Whatever that is or supposed to mean. Plato and Aristotle identify theology as paganism. Don't be misanthropic and antisocial, preferring the Last comers to the Original or First comers. You are not that ID they give you. You are not that passport they give you. You are not that driver's license they give you. You are not that social security number they give you. You are not that so-called birth certificate they give you. You are not that name or label or title they give you. You are the Creator. You are the Supreme Being. You are Neter and Netert. This they will not enlighten you on, because they themselves cannot be enlightened. They cannot enlighten or teach you what they are not. A carpenter only can teach and enlighten you to be a carpenter. Anything else a carpenter tries to teach different from carpentry is fraud. You are Neter and Netert.

Chapter 9: You Are the Universe

Stepping out on the journey of rediscovering of you are the Universe, have you ever felt lost, seeking approval and validation from the environment and surrounding around you?

Thus, we often look externally, wishing to find the universe, peace, happiness, and love.

You are the Universe, it is within you. We think that true joy comes from achieving certain goals and professions. Thinking that once attained our life will be filled with tranquility. However, does lasting happiness truly come from external achievements?

Hence, we all have moments where we feel our souls (remember, some don't have souls) tapestry seems incomplete. We revert to romantic social partners thinking they hold the missing pieces to our puzzle. This idea that another Neter and Netert is in competition with each other captivating yet fragile illusion.

Hence, amid these thoughts, we come to realize that chasing external desires is like trying to hold on to someone drowning, our brainwashing always hungry for wealth, riches, intimacy, position, luxury, and recognition is on a constant quest and a big illusion. However, these cosmos treasures are shiny, as they might be, all but fragments of delusions of grandeur truth.

Our heart and mind seek more with each fleeting pleasure, suggesting that true fulfillment is beyond what the cosmos can offer.

Thus, the universe doesn't want you to chase it. The Universe wants you to realize that you are already it.

And just Be!

Stop chasing the things you want. You are implying that they are running away from you. Instead, become the things you want and attract them. That's the only way you can get what you want. If you are the universe, comprehend that you have everything already.

So stop acting like you don't.

If you know you have what you want already by The Law of Nature those things will begin to appear in your physical reality. But any amount of doubt will slow the process down. Know that you are not in the Universe, you Are the Universe.

Chapter 10: You Are Everything

Have you not known that you have created everyone around you, and you created them in your mind, and that's including yourself. The truth is, nobody exists, including the character you think yourself to be.

Thus, if you are seeking the truth of what you truly are well stick around and really listen to what I am about to talk about. So, I'll first touch on the topic of Separation. If you can comprehend this, the remainder of this chapter will be very clear for you to see. However, just know that separation doesn't exist. The concept of separation is also a creation of the mind.

It's an illusion!

Now, you may say of course there is separation. Yes, you can have your opinions. You may also say, I am Heru, so how could I be my best friend Jok?

To tell you the truth, those are created characters produced from the mind. However, I have seeing a lot of you struggle with the concept of Oneness and how separation is an illusion. It is because they are constantly comparing the body and the mind, to other body and minds, and then they use distance as proof for separation. But Oneness is much more deeper than those things. First of all, you are not the body and mind. You are not the life you are experiencing. You are not your opinions and beliefs. What you are is vital life force itself.

Hence, from the perspective of what you truly are, you are the source of everything. So, think about everything that's connected to life. Nature is a part of life. The Male and Female body is a part of life experience. Negative emotions and thoughts are all a part of life. Life is everything and it's what you truly are. And through life experiences and social media etc., etc., we have all forgotten what we are, and we all have forgotten that everything is connected.

Now, here is another way of looking at it. What you are is Pure Consciousness. Not the body, not the mind. So don't you compare these to what you are. What I am is Consciousness! But we aren't individual consciousness. Consciousness has no form, and it has no shape, nor it cannot be located. We are this Consciousness as One. However, each vessel is just used for experiencing a different experience. The body and mind you are experiencing is just another perspective for consciousness to experience itself. So that it can learn and evolve. Ancient Alkebulan Neter and Netert were and always aware of Oneness.

And they were aware that the more Neter and Netert at a young age realize what they truly are the higher the collective consciousness will ascend.

Thus, this is why the Earth's vibrations was a lot higher back then. I am one hundred percent sure, this is how they have access to communication with their high dimensional Self-knowledge. Because they were able to vibrate on the same frequency with Oneness.

However, what we are is Consciousness. It's the mind that tells you another story. You have to realize that the mind has its own reality and outside of the mind is where real life is. And the mind creates separation. The mind has created others, and I can shortly and strongly explain.

The moment you meet someone, automatically a mental creation of them has begun. It may begin by just judging them or it may compare them. It begins throwing labels onto them, and now it has a character attached to that body and mind. However, let's say you go and chat to someone about this Netert you just met, to someone that already knows that Netert.

Now, you are telling them how that Netert are and how you perceive that Netert, and your friend that you are telling about the Netert that you meet, has a completely different perspective of that Netert. How is that possible? How can I perceive someone as confident and outgoing and outspoken and fun to be around, and another Netert sees them as cocky and know it all and knowing and energy draining to be around. It's because we think others are, isn't even what they truly are. It's all a creation of the mind.

Personality is created, you didn't come to Earth with it. And everyone is a reflection of you, I mean everyone. If you hate something about someone it's because they trigger something within you. It has nothing to do with them. If you are focused on yourself, hate wouldn't even be an energy within you.

Thus, there is literally no such thing as someone else. We are all pebbles of the same rock stone. We just act as if we are separate. But to actually experience Oneness, you must first realize that you yourself don't actually exist.

You must see that the character you think yourself to be is also a creation of the mind. You also may hear others say kill the Self-pride, detach from the Self-pride. The character you think yourself to be, lives within the Self-pride who you think you are, is just a collection of thoughts. Realize how the story of your life only exists within the mind through memories and imaginations. None of it is actually real. To see what's real, you have to see what's left when the mind isn't active.

However, the only thing that is happening is life. Thus life is one thing, and it's the only thing that's truly happening. You just don't realize it yet, because you are living through the mind and it's an illusion. Everything is living in a completely different reality. It's like we are all dreaming inside of one big collective dream. For example, how it is that some of you are afraid of snakes. Some of you can't watch snakes on a plane. Some of you may not like Animal Planet. Snakes just trigger your nerves of fear within you. Yet in my reality I love snakes. I usually have two of my own at the house and even pictures drawn all over my walls. How is that possible? Well, it's because we have created two different realities for our experiences, and that's only possible through the mind.

Thus, I think by now, you all should realize how truly powerful we are. It's so much deeper than we think. We are Everything.

We are Creators.

Very Powerful Creators. So powerful that we create characters and made them feel so real, that we completely abandon our true Nature and now think we are something we are not. That's how powerful the illusion of self is. But it's actually not our fault. We were programmed and conditioned this way by our parents, the news, schools, and society, and social media.

Thus, we must revert back to being empty of all labels and concepts. Totally, go back to what you were before the Cosmos told you who you are. So once you notice that you are not that character and can see how the mind creates these amazing illusions, you'll begin to realize that everyone else is stuck in this illusion. Meaning you will no longer perceive separation. Because you know that what you are is exactly what everyone else is. You will see that you are literally everyone and everything. Even when you begin thinking about someone, you are thinking about their character.

But the character doesn't actually exist.

Thus, yes, there is a body and mind, but who you think they are, is simply just another thought.

Noticing this will also allow you to emotionally detach from others. Because you aren't actually attached to them. You are attached to the thoughts about them. You are attached to who you think they are. But there is nobody. The only thing here is life. There is nobody here. It's all just life happening. Everything is One, and we are the Source of it All.

So remember you are Everything.

Chapter 11: Everything is Energy

Everything is energy and that's all there to it. Connect the puzzle to the frequency of the reality you wish, and you cannot help but to get that reality. Everything in the Cosmos is composed of energy.

Thus, have you ever thought about the idea that you too are a form of energy? It's easy to overlook, but you and me are constantly immersed in and inter-connected with energy. In fact, we are experiencing this connection even as we are reading this chapter. Every move we make, whether going to the park and drag or taking a deep breath, requires energy. Even our emotions and thoughts, ranging from joy to confusion, are forms of energy that can influence our experiences and impact the Cosmos around us.

However, taking the moment to truly comprehend that everything is energy can provide new insights about ourselves and the Cosmos. We are not separate from this energy. In fact, we are composed of it. Every part of our physical body, including our growth from our youth, the food we consume, and even our hair and nails is created up of energy. Energy flows through us, from the blood that circulates through our body, to the emotions and ideas that make up who we are.

Thus, we breathe it in and out with each breath. Energy envelops us and is in perpetual motion. Energy is not restricted to the physical realm alone.

It also encompasses our thoughts and emotions, which can influence our life and those of others.

What we perceive, what we meditate on, what we concentrate on, it is all a considerable amount of energy. Even the words we speak carry energy with them. What we watch on TV, or the internet is where we are investing our energy. Be mindful of what we invest our energy in, because it flows where our attention goes. It's always our decision where we choose to channel our energy. We have the option to choose our way of life well.

Thus, even making that decision consumes energy.

We have the authority to direct this energy, to decide where to concentrate it and how to employ it. By doing this, we can manage and guide it better toward our objectives and ambitions. Our energy moves in different directions whether you or I desire it or not, and our thoughts and emotions have the capacity to direct it.

However, when we experience joy, positivity, or motivation, we are releasing high frequency energy that brings more of the same to us. On the contrary, unfavorable emotions like frustration, unease, or melancholy draw low frequency energy that can drag us down. It's essential to realize that you possess the ability to control your energy.

When we feel down, we can shift our focus to something that elevates our mood. We can also adjust our energy by spending moments with Neter and Netert who uplift us, pursuing activities that we enjoy, and surrounding ourselves with constructive messages. We can also take measures to preserve our energy by setting boundaries, avoiding harmful circumstances and relationships, and engaging in self-care practices.

Thus, have you ever wondered what happens to our energy when we put our trust and loyalty in something? The cosmos conspires in our favor to bring us everything our energy attracts. Trusting and having loyalty in the power of energy can transform our lives in amazing ways. By trusting in energy, we acknowledge our worthiness to receive and the generosity to give to others.

We begin to see that there is more to life than what meets the eye, and that there is a greater force in us. We become a part of something much greater, something that knows everything, comprehends everything, and is an infinite source of love. When we trust, our energy aligns, our cells rejuvenate, and mental health and physical health improves. Despair, confusion and disappointment all dissipate, leaving us feeling more serene, balanced and weightless.

Hence, our energy becomes clear, pure, and flows like the River Nile. We feel valuable and deserving, and joy fills our life. We gain wisdom and knowledge comprehensiveness, and inner peace, and clarity fills our soul. This is the power of energy, and when we trust in it, everything falls into place. When we trust in the Cosmos and have loyalty in our own potential, our energy becomes more potent, yet lighter. Wisdom, knowledge and comprehension and serenity flow within our soul.

However, our thoughts become beliefs and our aspirations flow in our life. By believing in our dreams and taking action towards them, we can transform our life and achieve everything we desire. Trust in yourself and in the cosmos to guide us towards our Divine purpose and we will unveil our true mission in this Cosmos. Once we comprehend and embrace Our Divine purpose, we will realize that we possess all the necessary tools to succeed, and we are capable of achieving our goals.

Thus, trusting helps us to let go of all the obstacles and resistance in our path. We embrace the present moment as it is, and we can see it with absolute clarity. We open our heart and mind to receive the wonders that the cosmos has in store for us. By trusting we allow ourselves to release the things that don't serve us and make way for new opportunities. When you trust, you have loyalty in the Divine Force that guides you, and you are never alone. You comprehend that you are part of something more significant than yourself, and you have a crucial role to play. You think that every event that occurs in your life is for your greater good, growth and development.

Thus, can you trust? Can you trust your energy?

Can you trust the cosmos? Can you trust yourself?

Try to close your eyes, connect with your inner self, and feel the energy that courses through you. Feel the love, the power, the light. We are energy and we possess the power to create our own reality and bring out our dreams. You are capable, deserving and adored.

Therefore, trust in yourself and in the Cosmos, and witness the magic that unfolds in your life. The power of trust and thinking in the Cosmos can have a transformative impact on our physical body, altering our energy.

Our thinking, thoughts, emotions and words can elevate in our environment and can even help heal our body. To turn your thoughts into thinking, it's essential to practice the act of thinking. By having loyalty in the cosmos ability to provide everything we need, knowing our potential, desires and dreams, and confident in your worthiness of love and happiness, you can experience profound peace and joy. Knowing that you have a purpose to fulfill in this Cosmos can help us realize and fulfill it.

Thus, we have the power to create the life we desire and shape our reality. But this requires intention, awareness, and practice. That journey begins by recognizing that we are energy and that we are always surrounded by it. Every breath, thought and movement is an expression of our energy when connected to the cosmos and its infinite intelligence. However, when we realize this connection, we comprehend that we are part of something much larger than livity itself.

Hence, we comprehend that there is a Divine purpose for our existence and that we have the power to fulfill it. We appreciate the precious gift of our energy and strive to use it wisely. We choose to focus on abundance, gratitude, and positivity instead of so-called fear, doubt, and lack. We cultivate a mindset of great thoughts, trust, and loyalty, and we practice it every chance we get. When we have loyalty and let go of the need to so-called control, worry or doubt, we are opening up to the infinite possibilities of the Cosmos.

Thus, we allow the free flow of energy to guide us, trusting that everything is unfolding for our greater dimension, even if we can't see it yet. We have unwavering loyalty in the Cosmos ability to provide what you and I need, and in our ability to attract it into our livity.

Every obstacle is an opportunity to grow, every setback is a lesson and for a greater comeback, and every challenge is a chance to become stronger and wiser. When we activate the power of our energy through thoughts, we are able to create wonders in our own livity.

Hence, we speak our truth with confidence and sincerity, visualize our dreams with clarity, and follow nothing but our intuition with courage. Our heart leads the way, and we trust in the long journey ahead. We comprehend that our energy is magnetic and that it attracts others, opportunities and experiences aligned with our desire. We are grateful for each moment, each Neter and Netert, and each lesson that comes our way. Recognizing that they all play a vital role in our livity journey. As we cultivate the skill of laboring with energy, we become the master of our destiny. We emanate positivity, happiness, and serenity. Hello, we motivate others to do the same. We effortlessly show our aspirations, and we give back to others with benevolence. We dwell in harmony with the natural Cosmos with others, and with our own self. We treasure the splendor of every instant, and we respect the wisdom in every obstacle.

Thus, we express gratitude for our energy, for the Cosmos, and for the ability of existence. Acknowledge in one own self becomes effortless through practice, and it is possible to develop this skill by reciting positive affirmations and feeling their truth resonate in our heart. Trusting in our creative abilities, imagination, and inner voice can help us find our Divine purpose in our livity and lead a rewarding and joyful existence. By placing our trust in ourselves and our connection to the cosmos, we can exude tranquility and love and make a positive impact on the cosmos around us.

However, when you trust you, approach challenges with a composed and focused mindset and heart. We are aware that no matter what comes our way, we can handle it with elegance and ease. We have loyalty in the process of levity and all of its twists, turns, ups, downs, and unexpected surprises.

We acknowledge that everything occurs for a reason, and each experience, whether positive or negative, presents a chance for growth and learning. We trust that the entire Cosmos is on our side and that everything will labor out for our own well-being. We also trust that the Neter and Netert in our livity way are there to support us and that we are not alone on our livity journey.

Thus, as we develop our trust, we will gain a deeper awareness of the energy that surrounds us. We will sense the vibrations of Neter and Netert and other things around us, and we will choose the energy that serves our greatest dimension. We will protect our energy and create healthy boundaries with those who do not align with our positive vibrations. Trusting also means embracing forgiveness for your own and others. Forgiveness is a powerful tool that releases negative energy and liberates us from the old.

We will let go of grudges and resentment and open our hearts and minds to new possibilities, that let our energy flow wide and deep because everything is Energy. Now, always remember and tell someone that we are all energy, and we have the ability to shape our own reality according to our own will and need. We have out there negative and positive energies.

So, let me drop you this jewel. When it comes to things like sexual intercourse energy exchange. It has been known that it takes a life period, after having sex or making love to someone, that you actually carry that someone's energy around. Thus, this is including their dramas, their traumas, their emotions, their feelings, their insecurities, their low par of self-esteem, or whatever else there may be in energy. So however, be very careful with whom you choose to share your energy with.

Because it's doing more harm than good to your physical health, mental health, consciousness, and energy than you could ever begin to imagine. However, to not put too much threat in front of this, I also want to say that what would happen if you would revert this around? Who and what is it that you are actually so inspired by that you would want to curry that someone negative energies around for decades?

Think about it!

Chapter 12: The Divine Purpose

Divine Purpose in all walks of our livity journey. The search for meanings and Divine Purpose has captivated our hearts and minds for decades. We find ourselves pondering the profound question. What is the main Divine Purpose in our levity journey?

No doubt we are Divine for real! This eternal inquiry stirs within us yearning to uncover the deeper significance behind our existence and to detect a sense of direction that transcends the mundane.

Thus, at the core of this exploration lies the remarkable journey of self-knowledge. Beckons us to peer beyond the veils of our conditioned identities and societal roles inviting us to question the illusion of the self. We have constructed in the realm of Divine Worship and self-growth. There is a growing recognition that true Divine Purpose lies not in external accomplishments or material possessions.

But in the awakening to our authentic nature to unravel the main Divine Purpose in our livity journey.

Thus, we must go beyond the limitations of our conceptual self. This illusory construct shaped by societal conditioning and external validation often lead us astray generating a persistent sense of lack and unfulfillment. The path to true Divine Purpose begins with recognizing our consciousness and that our worth does not derive from the transient opinions or achievements dictated by the cosmos around us.

However, when we surrender the power to define our worth to the cosmos, we relinquish our Sovereignty and become subject to its judgments.

We place our Freedom, Happiness and fulfillment in the hands and cares of external forces. Forever chasing an elusive dream of acceptance and validation. Yet the cosmos criteria for worth are fleeting and ever-changing. Leaving us perpetually dissatisfied and unfulfilled. Within this conceptual framework we may find ourselves trapped forever.

Seeking external validation and constantly striving for achievements that never truly satisfy our deepest longing. By living at the par of our physical senses we lake ourselves to be the physical body and mind. When we vide ourselves in this manner, we say that we are a mind and body that have a soul.

Thus, our activities all along are focused on nurturing and providing for the body. The significance of self-awaken lies in unraveling these layers of conditioning and peeling back the facade of the conceptual self. It involves a willingness to question the narratives we have internalized and to embark on an inward journey of exploration and reflection. By shinning the light of awareness on our thoughts, emotions and thinking we begin to unveil the illusionary nature of the self we have clung to for so long. Transcending the illusion of the self is not a negation of our oneself or a rejection of our unique experience.

We have been given this experience and it is therefore correct that we play this game to the best of our knowledge as Neter and Netert.

However, it's nice to achieve something in this moment of levity, but it cannot tell you who and what you are. So, transcending this illusion is an awakening to a deeper truth that lies beyond and the limited construct of the pride of self.

It is recognizing that our Essence is not confined to the roles we play, the titles we hold, or the achievements we accumulate. When we fully embrace our true Nature and connect with the forever Essence that exists beyond the ever-changing nature of the external Cosmos, our true Divine Purpose reveals itself. Loss often serves as a catalyst for this awakening, a doorway through which we enter into a deeper comprehension of ourselves and our place in this Cosmos. Losing can be a blessing for some. It is in moment of profound loss, when our attachments are severed, that we are confronted with the impermanence of livity and the fragility of our identities.

Thus, these experiences can initiate a profound inner journey awakening to truths that were previously obscured. When we experience significant loss, whether it be the loss of a loved one, are cherished relationship, a so-called career, or a prized possession, it shakes the very foundations of our identity. And the attachments we held dear are transitory in nature. This confrontation can propel us into a space of introspection, inviting us to question who we truly are, beyond these external trappings. While the loss of attachments and the dismantling of fictitious identities can be painful and disorienting. They also present us with a profound opportunity for growth and gratitude. In the wake of loss, gratitude emerges as a guiding force. We develop an appreciation for the impermanence of levity. Cherishing each moment as a gift. We learn to cultivate gratitude not only for what we have experienced and gained. But also for what we have released and let go. Through this practice of gratitude, we foster a deep sense of contentment and find solace in the realization that true fulfillment arises not from external possessions or achievements. But from an inner alignment with our authentic selves.

Hence, the power of awareness is a profound power that lies within each one of us. Practicing present moment awareness allows us to top into a state of deep presence and connection with the unfolding reality of each moment. It is in this state of awareness that we can truly awaken to the richness and beauty of livity. Present moment awareness is the practice of being fully attentive to the Here and Now. Without getting caught up in regrets of some so-called past or worries about the so-called future by bringing our attention to the present moment we open ourselves to the fullness of our experiences, the sights sounds, smells, and sensations that surround us. It is through this heightened awareness that we can rediscover something deeper as an emerged.

However, now in this present moment surrender yourself to the experience of pure listening. Have you not perceived the profound difference it holds?

Who and what truly lives within you? Are you only the selfish mind, that until moments ago, incessantly judged, pondered over the so-called past and fretted over the uncertainties of the so-called future or is there something more behind these guises you see?

Through this process we can transcend the surface level identity. Hence, you are now awakening. The universe is awakening through us all. The universe is listening to itself. Trying to find the meaning of livity with words is like trying to sing a song by describing it you're missing the point. If you want to know the meaning of livity, sit back for a while on an old iron bridge above a calm river in the country area in late autumn. Feel the cool breeze glide across your skin. Listen clearly to the sounds of the forest quietly singing to itself, in dove song. See how the light goes yellow, red, blue and purple as the sun dips down below the horizon. In this livity this is all the meaning you will ever get, but it is all the meaning that you could ever need to know what is your true Divine Purpose. One of our biggest lack of knowledge of self is that the Male Neter do not know that they have a Divine purpose, and the Female Netert do not know that they are sacred and have a Divine Purpose too.

Hence, all Male Neter must know that they have a Divine Purpose, not to cohabit with non-virgin females.

Why Neter should only cohabit with a virgin? Many non-virgin Females will start hating on me reading this chapter and book. But I don't care.

Because their evil and wicked practices exposed. I will just keep on exposing the truth.

There's been all kinds of studies that reveal that when a Female sleeps around, she is less likely to stay married or happily married.

- Marrying a virgin gives Males a 99.99 percent chance of a happy marriage.
- Virgins are far less emotionally dangerous and damage, and drama and trauma free, far less combative, can still pair bond with their Male partner, more submissive, better for long term relationships, kinder and way more purer for their Male partner.
- A high value self-confident Male should not want to marry or cohabit with a Female who wasted her prime youth on somebody else. What are you, a garbage disposal?
- Non-Virgin Females are like carrying trial and crosses from previous relationships.
- Virgins are more open to experiences and adventures.
- Virgins have less emotional scars which means healthy and productive relationships.
- You don't want to raise someone else's child, create your own daycare.
- Virgin will look up to you and make you feel your true Divine Purpose as a Neter.

- Virgins are far more attractive, more beautiful, more fun, and they are more happier.
- The more Male partners she sleeps with the more her character, value, worth, and self-esteem decrease. This is where she changes from a Netert, and be called a woman, lady, whore, or prostitute. She sells her Divine Purpose and Sacred womb for sexual pleasure and sex gain.
- When you are the experienced one, she will desire you more.
- The sex is meaningful for the Virgin Females, unlike the experienced one.

Now, why would a Neter go for a 30-year-old Female, when he can have a fresh 21-year-old virgin Netert?

She's 30, which means she's older, she's ran through, she's tarnished, and she's hardened by all the relationships, so she lost her femininity. It's very unfortunate that Females don't realize that until they hit their 30s, they want to be in their twenties and be like oh yeah, I can have intercourse with this Male and that Male and so. This is disrespectful to our ancestors. But they don't realize they are ruining themselves. And then they're trying to find themselves, and by the time they are thirty they are asking where have all the good Male gone?

Definitely not to you because you ran through.

This is the cause and effect and the main source of all Females unhappiness, bitterness and dissatisfaction. If her first lover didn't make her happy and satisfied, how are you going to make her?

Thus, this is where they turn their Divine Gifted Purpose, in to evil and wickedness.

Female virginity was of utmost important in the Ages of our Alkebulan forefathers and foremothers. If female went to her marriage bed having already engaged in illicit, or sexual intercourse with anyone but her husband, she would be considered as a 'whore' and would likely be stone to death or otherwise be treated as an outcast, by her family and friends. This concept needs to be at present, to stop all the vices, evil, and wickedness.

Hence, the lifespan of a Male sperm inside of a Female vagina goes like this. Healthy Male sperm can live forever after sexual intercourse. Since time and space are an illusion, we cannot use hours or dates because we only have Now. The life span of the Male sperm inside the Female vagina depends entirely on the environment they are in. The specificities of the Female's uterus, vagina, and fallopian tubes determine the lifespan of the Male sperm inside of her. Having a fertile cervical fluid will increase the survival rates of the Male sperm inside the Female Vagina.

The Vaginal canal in Females is acidic in nature and only the healthiest of the Male sperm will survive that moment they have sexual intercourse.

Each moment a Male ejaculate, are 100 billion sperm is been released through his semen. Only a few sperm will survive the tough trip through the Female vagina and into the fallopian tubes. The ones that reach the cervical fluid can safely survive, move towards the fallopian tubes and await the arrival of the egg from the ovaries for that present moment.

Thus, so, having one sexual partner is also vaginal hygiene. Each Male a Female put inside of her from the first Male with whom she had sexual intercourse to take her virginity, and all others after him are committing an act of homosexuality. All those that are after her first is having sex on another male sperm that lasts for eternity inside of her. And this wicked homosexual act must be stopped. Each Male Sperm last inside her after ejaculates inside her for the rest of her life. You are actually having sex onto another Male penis sperm that never leaves her vagina. Thus, this is why all Neter must find him a virgin Netert and be with her for life.

So please spread this knowledge, and let's put an end to that kind of secret homosexuality act from used or non-virgin female. This will end the act of stepchildren and the so-called act of cheating. They only become women, ladies, prostitutes, whores, etc., because they are non-virgin, and once they are virgins they are Netert. We all are gifted with a Divine Purpose. And all Netert was gifted with a sacred womb. And the Neter who has the nucleus of life, supposed to be gifted with sacred sperm too. Yet because this kind of knowledge self-have been hidden from us for so long, our Females allows all kinds of different Male sperm to enter her sacred womb and vagina. Look at it from any point of view you want to. It's by mixing all these sperm into your vagina and sacred womb is what creates all these Evilous Children, that don't know the way of life of a Neter and Netert.

They have known that their Divine Purpose has established a way of life for us to live and eat healthy. Look at all Neter and Netert cosmos wide and know that a bit of good living and intellectual development for all of us can score off our list three quarters of the patients and three quarters of the diseases.

The cemeteries and the hospitals would be empty. Look at some of us, we do not have a dry and well-ventilated bedroom much less a house. Dash away physic to all the dogs! Fresh clean air, good diet - vegan or Blue Zone diet, a little bit of exercise in the country area, less crushing labor - that is exactly how we must begin. Without this, the whole profession of a so-called doctor is nothing but trickery and humbug. And this is the way of life of a true Divine Purpose that we must rediscover.

Hence, I advise you all to utilize your Divine Purpose and use your power to know the danger of sugar, meat and seafood to your health. Please heal and cure yourself and prevent these:

(1)   Sugar in a baby's brain is called ADHD.
(2)   Sugar in an adult brain is called dementia and Alzheimer's.
(3)   Sugar in your teeth is called cavities.

(4)   Sugar in your eyes is called glaucoma

(5)   Sugar on your skin is called aging.

(6)   Sugar in your sleep is called insomnia.

(7)   Sugar in your blood is called diabetes.

(8)   Excess sugar in your system is called Cancer.

(9)   Sugar on Wall Street is called a billion-dollar industry.

Addiction to sugar is eight times, eight times more powerful than cocaine! I am not saying that you cannot eat natural sugar from your fruits and vegetables. But what I am saying is that you must know what your real enemy is.

(10) Now all kinds of meats and sea food cause cancer, diabetes and toxoplasma. Toxoplasmosis is also linked to unwashed fruits, unwashed vegetables, and contaminated water. Toxoplasma is mainly linked to fish and shrimp, crawfish and lobster. Be careful and know the enemy!

Now, how can or how could you say you are a high value Female or Male, or Netert or Neter or have a Divine Purpose and depending on some so-called doctor or physician to help you or cure you? Also, here is something else to think about. How could or how can you say or claim that you are a high value Female or high value Male or have a Divine Purpose and depending on to punch someone else clock to work or keep a 9 to 5 job? Do you think high value Females and high value Males and Divine Purpose Neter and Netert hold jobs at Walmart, K-Mart, Kentucky Fried Chicken etc., etc.? High value Female and Male and Divine Purpose Neter and Netert need hair wigs, hair straightening creams, face make-ups, and fingers and toenail extensions? Get the heck out of here! Are you for real? Are you truly serious?

How could or how can you be or have high value or possess Divine Purpose when you all possess a man-made education?

Now, here is a trick and deceit to your high value and Divine Purpose. They brainwashed you to a song that goes like this: God made man, and man made money, God made the bees, and the bee made honey, he made the devil, and the Devil made sin. Thus, looking into that song real good, and see what man-made, and say to yourself how could I be high value or have a Divine Purpose and chasing down man-made material things and money and goods? Have you ever used an etymological dictionary to etymology the words: God, Man, Devil, and Money and Sin?

The World's First bible reveals God is the Devil.

I have pointed it out in many chapters in this book. So, you high value and Divine Purpose claimers, please be mindful and heartful of these hidden Truth. I recommend you all to the etymology of the words God, Devil, Man, Sin, Human, Human being, Person, Job, and Work. You can also utilize: An

Egyptian Hieroglyphic Dictionary volume one and two, edited by E. A. Wallis Budge.

There, is my last message to you all who call or profess to be high value or have a Divine Purpose, before I close this chapter. How can you be high value or possess Divine Purpose when you all putting your mouth down on each other private parts? Don't you know that's Sodomy or Homosexuality?

Thus, here I will use an etymological dictionary and etymology the word; Sodomy, for you all.

Sodomy: "Sodomie, unnatural sexual relations"... especially between men but also with beasts, from Old French Sodomie. Compare Late Latin peccatum "anal sex," literally the sin of Sodom," from Latin Sodomy noun: (1) anal or oral copulation with another person especially: anal or oral copulation with a member of the same sex (2) Copulation with an animal."

My beloved Neter and Netert, please know and acknowledge your Divine Purpose in you and stop being deceived and tricked and brainwashed and misled by the Devil's way of life. Lastly, here is a little bit of Divine Purpose of conscious sexual education, self-knowledge to abolish your mind manipulating whoring, prostituting, and gold-digging mentality.

Thus, remembering at all moments that gold digging comes in all forms and shapes. However, this is a confused and perverted cosmos we all live in. One generation of Netert wants a Neter with a big penis, and one generation of Neter wants a Netert with a tight vagina. This is a big curse and insult to the Creator, like it is you who create your own body and do the artwork on each body parts! Yet both Neter and Netert are confused to think that a Netert vagina is one size fits all the penis in the cosmos. No, that is far from it. That is where we lower the value and worth in our Netert and turn them into whores, prostitutes, and gold diggers.

Thus, all Netert who want or looking for a Neter with a big or long penis, is also considered a gold digger. And a Neter who requests to find a Netert with a tight vagina, and fat vagina, is also called a gold digger.

Hence, there are about 8 different types of vaginas, and none of them are big or too small. So be pleased and happy with what the Creator provided for you or what has been created for you to have in this Cosmos. Please be satisfied and content with what you have or got, and do not curse the Creator by saying the Creator creates inequality- one big and one small, and one tight, and one loose.

Thus, these are some of the names of the various types of vaginas:

(1)   Bare down there
(2)   Long and lovely
(3)   Bold and Bushy
(4)   Asymmetrical
(5)   The confident clitoris
(6)   The full mound

(7)   Decorated down there
(8)   Darker Drapery.

Hence, here are the two different types of penises:

(1)   Grower
(2)   Shower

The average penis size when erected is 5-1/2 inches, and the size when shrunk is about 2 inches. And the longest both grower and shower can get is 6-1/2 inches, and as I said above, the shortest both might can get is 3 inches, and the girth of both of them is any way from 2-1/2 inches.

Hence, vaginal compatibility to a Neter grower penis or shower penis shape and size. A true, genuine, and authenticated Netert vagina can achieve the right fit and feelings with a true, genuine, and authenticated Neter grower or shower penis. If the first time a Netert have sex in her life with a Neter, and that Neter has a grower penis or shower penis, which ever penis that Neter has, that is the type of penis that Netert must have sex with during all her life span, upon this earth. If she crosses them up, she is not a Netert, and she does not have a Divine Purpose. Once she crosses them up, she is going to go through life chasing penises after the penises, to try to find that first fit and feelings and happy pleasure from that first experience.

Thus, it doesn't matter how hard you search for sizes of penises and tightness of vaginas, just remember that sexual pleasure has nothing to do with procreation and self-respect and self-value, and self-worth.

Hence, seasonings such as they called New Moon, and Full Moon have a lot to do with one's penis and vagina. At New Moon, a Neter penis always reaches its full length and girth, and the Netert vagina shrinks to its regular size, and that is when you all produce a Male Neter baby. And when it is Full Moon the Neter penis shrinks, and the Netert vagina swell to its full size (some call it fat) and that is when you produce a Female Netert baby.

Hence, those are the only two ways a Netert can get pregnant -- New Moon and Full Moon. You can try some more, or longer sex, it will never happen. Now, since many Netert consider that long sex is bored and jade, in the same place all that while, just remember your Divine purpose, that any Neter can make a Netert have an orgasm one or two or three times in little and no time -- as in three minutes. The sensitive spot is 2 inches up under the front of the vagina.

Hence, just learn from the above self-knowledge who and what you are, and you have the different types of penises and vaginas to master. Neter, I must say that a Netert wants you to know that sensitive spot and do touch that sensitive spot that makes her have an orgasm, which they erroneously call G-spot, that makes her wet and cum how many times you want her to cum, so she can feel lovable, release her stress, pain and feel good within herself, where the sex can be more fun and pleasurable for both of you that none of you weak in the waist, and strong in the face. Stop being delusional.

94

Hence, the location of the sensitive orgasm spot (so-called G-spot) is typically exposed as being about 2 to 3 inches) inside the vagina, on the front upper wall. For all Netert, so longs their Neter has 2 or 3 inches of penis to stimulate this area of the vagina, it will create a more intense orgasm, than any kind of fore playing with the clitoral stimulation.

Hence, teach this Divine Purpose, and knowledge to the younger generation, to end gold digging, foreplay, and changing your partners like you change your draws.

Chapter 13: Time, Space, Past and Future are all an Illusion, Only the Present is Real

Thus, there are some cunning ones, who have brainwashed you into thinking that there is 24 hours in a day, and 12 months is a year, so you all agree to give those cunning ones 8 hours a day of their forced labor that they force upon you.

Now tell me what the heck is night, if it is 24 hours in one day? They will never educate you to know that it is only 12 hours would and can be in a day, and 7 days in one week, 28 days in one month, and 13 months in a year, because then you would get smart and wouldn't give them 8 hours on their force labor.

1+11= 12	4+8=12	6+6=12
2+10=12	5+7=12	
3+9=12	8+4=12	

Total of 6 hours in a Day

It is also 7 days would be made up a week, and 28 days would be made up a month, instead of 30 and 31 days.

7 days = one week.

28 days = one month.

28 x12=336 days would be in a year.

They make you think that it is 364 or 365 days in one year. That's a lie!

364 - 336=28

336 + 28=364

Do you see that, that it is 13 months in one year, if you go by it the correct way by 7 days per week, 28 days per month, and 12 months at 28 days, it would add up to 336 days per year, which would leave one extra 28 days, from the original 364 days per year that you were brainwashed to.

At present it's 13 months in the year you striving to kill yourself into their slavery.

Night is Grand rising. Grand rising time is Night, too.

Time is nothing but an illusion. Now this can be the most awesome breakdown of time that you probably will ever be heard about time being an illusion.

Because of your tradition and indoctrination most of you will not grasp the truth of it, no matter how hard I try or what I try or what I do. Some of you will get it. Days is an illusion. Months is an illusion.

Years is an illusion. That makes birthdays and all other days an illusion.

Thus, anything which cannot be brought to a trial is, for that reason alone, impossible to be determined, there exists no rule, no term of comparison, no means of certainty, respecting them.

Ok, so, now let me reveal to you how time is an illusion. Now, really if you think about it and say what is truly time? So, when we say time, what do we mean, and what are we measuring? We are actually measuring the sun revolves around a centre just as the earth revolves around the sun. That's the first thing. And this was stolen the wrong way from the Alkebulan Neter and Netert, to deceive you into some time hoax.

However, when we are measuring time, when 12 PM hit at what they called midnight or nighttime, we see that one day ended, and another day started. And this day ends, and day start, it still based on the traveling of the sun. Because this is when the Sun revolves around a centre just as the earth revolves around the sun. And in its speed and droppings we say midnight to twelve, and then at 6, that's when it's rising up. Then at the other 6 that's when it set 12:00 to 12:00, and 6:00 to 6:00. It is all based on the cycle of the sun.

Hence, and there you go. That is how they get the time that you so preciously worship. Time is based on the traveling on the sun. However, comprehend that if we looking at time, if it is at 11:59 and you are looking at your (watch), like oh yeah, the day is about to end, touch down it, then hit 12:00 o'clock. Did the day really ended? No! No, it did not. Did anything ended?

No! There is no really such thing as a one-day to the next day. That is the illusion within the mind, programmed in you from your youth, by evil and the wicked ones who come up with the time hoax. We are just following the sun they indoctrinated in us to follow.

However, it's even go way deeper into the recycle madness. Right about now, we would say that it is the year 2018 C.E. Now, if you go back two thousand eighteen so-called years to zero. That would not be the beginning of the cosmos.

No, way, that is not the beginning of the so-called time. Who started this crazy madness over?

Hence, when we looked into the Alkebulan Neter and Netert knowledge, and all of their philosophy and the so-called philosophy days of the so-called Greeks and Pythagoras days, that is before the zero point. Now, tell me how this so-called time starts all over? What the heck is it, is it not 2018? To me, it's all an illusion that has been programed into our minds from our youth, in our homes and their schools and colleges and universities.

So, none of you can deny that time is not a fraud or fake.

Hence, let's fathom one step down more into revealing to you how time is really fake. When talk about the past, there is no such thing as the past. It, too, is an illusion. Can you tell me and show me what is the past? That is when I will take heed. Now, what is the Past? Right now, me talking and writing this will be considered as the past. But have you not looking what is happening right now is this present.

Thus, all this moments that we have been calling the past is just our memory of the present moment. There is really no past! Because if you and I don't remember the present moment, then you and I won't and will not have any past. So taking away that memory, there will be no past. That, past is just a memory. That just shows you that it is something mental.

Thus just ask yourself now, what is the future then? Some of you might say tomorrow is the future. Yet when tomorrow comes, when will it happen? It still going to happen in the present moment. We will not, going to experience tomorrow, tomorrow. I say to you, we will all experience it now! Therefore, we know that this future is just us program to projecting our mind into something that is supposed to be ahead of us.

Which is not. It's just a big illusion.

However, when we get there, it all happens in the present moment. That is how you know that there are no such things as the past, and there is no such thing as the future either. They are all happening at the same present moment. How can anyone with common sense deny that? Hence, it's only a present moment. The present moment is you and I, and the entire Cosmos around you and I, and you and I in it! Shut your eyes and, then open them up, it's still the present moment. Let's just say, your loved ones woke up from their sleep in their catacombs, they will see the same present moment and its essence, as a young baby coming into his or her senses to know the names of the things around them. That is all that is existed! The past and present and future exist at the same moment.

Space. Space may seem like a simple idea. Some things are here, and some things are there, and there is a distance between them. That is it, we don't really think of space as a thing. It is just the back dropping which everything else just happens. But what exactly separates here from there?

Thus, we have learned from some contemporary scholars that the distance between two objects depends on who you ask. An observer moving at close to the speed of light and one standing still will disagree about how far apart two points in space are as you get closer to the speed of light. Distant strengths and here and there get closer to becoming just the same place. But this gets weirder.

Hence, contemporary scholars, also showed that mass and energy bend space and time, and that is what we experience as gravity in this view space and time sort of rest on top of the gravitational field, created by the mass and energy in the cosmos. The problem is this, happy arrangement breaks down, when you try to apply it at really small scales, where quantum effects take hold. Crazy as it may sounds, we don't actually have a concept of space that's has been proven to work for both the galaxies and quarks. But there are some assumptions. One idea called loop quantum.

Gravity views space and time as lumpy. The result of a vast network of knots, braids and twists that carry information. One link in the network might correspond to say an electron. While a different one a few links away might be a quark. The connectedness of the network determines how, when and where. Particles interact giving rise to what we perceive as space and time. A different idea called causal sets, views space and time as just a vast collection of instances rather than being a random jumble.

Thus, these single events are linked by causality. If you take them as a whole, the idea of space and time is sort of like how the concept of temperature emerges from the motion of many particles acting together.

These aren't the only ideas that might explain what space is and where it comes from. And no one do not know whether if any of them are correct. But they all point to a common or single source. Space is not a fundamental part of what we choose to call reality. It arises from something else. Something to really ponder upon, next moment you're trying to get from here to there. Because you will not find a here or there, and you will not find anything from now as space, because space is an illusion.

Conclusion

Our final conclusion, with this book, and for this masterpiece, is to see and know and hear that this book and its knowledge reaches about ten million Alkebulan Neter and Netert around this Cosmos. To transform all ten million readers who purchase this book and whoever they recommend it to, back into their rightful gifted natural conscious state of mind and heart. So, they know who and what they truly are. They then can assist to spread this book and its knowledge to continue awakening 10 million more Alkebulans Neter and Netert. This is our only true and correct protest, awaken, revolution, war, religion, job, work, law, money, unity, education, common sense, equality, freedom, liberty, justice and consciousness.